La Caja China

Smoke!

Real BBQ in the Magic Box

Perry P. Perkins

La Caja China: Smoke!

Real BBQ in the Magic Box

Published by:

Elk Mountain Books

Longview, WA 98632

editor@elkmountianbooks.com

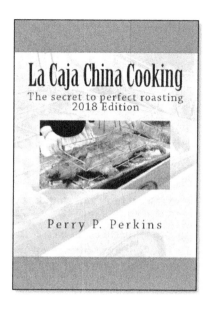

La Caja China World

Roasting Box Recipes from Around the Globe

In "La Caja China Cooking", we took you on a gastronomic tour of America.

With this new collection of recipes, your La Caja China becomes a magic carpet, allowing you to take your friends and family to the far corners of the world, and experience the delicious wonders waiting for you there!

In every culture and country that we researched in gathering this collection, we found people who enjoyed gathering together with loved ones, lighting a fire, cooking meat over it (or under it), and eating together.

Not coincidentally, we think, these folks shared a common passion for life and laughter, as well.

In "La Caja China World", we invite your tastebuds to join us on a globe-trotting adventure with dishes like:

~ Grilled Tri-Tip & Chimichurri in Argentina

~ Whole Roast Pig & Coconut Rice in Bali

~ Roast lamb & Potatoes in Greece

~ Beef Short Ribs & Scallion Salad in Korea

~ Christmas Goose in Sweden

If you're looking for a means to roast, grill, bake, braise, smoke, or barbecue, whether you're cooking for a hungry crowd, or creating memories with your family - look no further than La Caja China Cooking!

US$14.95

Available at: www.perryperkinsbooks.com

La Caja China Party!

Making Memories with the Magic Box

La Caja China is not a good or a service – It's an experience.

It's a culture. It's about the age-old mainstays of good food, good friends, and good times. It's rugged but romantic.

Requiring butchering, braising, brining and handling.

It's charcoal and chatter.

As the food cooks, the aromas become as enticing as the spectacle itself. It becomes not just a conversation piece, but a conversation starter.

Chef-tested and fully-illustrated party themes.

Insider tips and tricks, and over 80 bbq & grilling recipes for the La Caja China roasting box!

US$14.95

Available at: www.perryperkinsbooks.com

La Caja China Grill!

Live Fire on the Magic Box

Grilling. It's the most primitive of all the cooking methods.

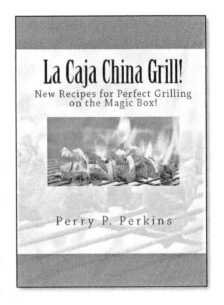

La Caja China Grill provides the roasting box owner with detailed instructions for both direct and indirect grilling, specifically on the "top grills" of the Cuban–style pig-roasting boxes and Cajun Microwaves, whose popularity have exploded with their exposure on Food Television, and with cooks and chefs like Bobby Flay, Andrew Zimmern, and Martha Stewart.

More than 70 delicious beef, pork, poultry, fish, and vegetable entrees for the grill, as well as sides, sauces, rubs, and everything the grill-master needs for the perfect flame-kissed meal.

All recipes are fully illustrated, and many provide web-links to additional cooking tips, definitions, and how-to videos.

Summer's coming! It's time to oil up those grills, fire up the coals…and make some magic! US$14.95

Available at: www.perryperkinsbooks.com

Table of Contents

Foreword

Why I Love My La Caja China

Quality

My first and foremost priority, when smoking, or any cooking, really…is the quality of the finished product.

I have a *lot* of grills and smokers (*don't get my wife started*!) and the meats that I roast or smoke in my Caja is every bit as good, and usually better, that any of my other grills or smokers.

Price

Unless I want to spend every spring hauling a bunch of cinder-blocks around, or digging pits in my yard, La Caja China is about the best value out there for roasting a one-hundred-pound pig.

I have a big pit smoker as well, and I can tell you this, you could buy 3-4 La Caja China's for the price of one of *those* monsters.

Ease of use

If you've ever had to flip a whole, cooked, hog on a grill, or in a pit…you'll take one look at La Caja China's "rack and hook" system, and never look back.

Not only can I flip my pigs by myself, I can flip them with one hand!

Portability

I've taken my Caja places that I wouldn't have dreamed of hauling a pit, or pellet, smoker…especially not one big enough for whole hogs.

It's the star of the show at our big family campout each summer, it's cooked many a dinner in elk camp each fall, and I never take a trip to the beach without it!

Because of its size, weight, and portability, I've been able to roast pigs for friend's birthdays, their kid's graduation parties, and even a couple of weddings!

K.I.S.S. (Keep it Simple…)

Whatever male gene that guys are born with that makes them handy with tools, good at repairing things, and able to work on their own cars...

Yeah, I didn't get ANY of them.

- *No moving parts*
- *No electricity*
- *No complicated start-up/shut down procedures*

For a three-thumbed klutz like me, they had me at "no moving parts"...

Flexibility

I'm a pretty creative chef, and I'm also highly ADHD, which means I need stuff around me that can ...*go with the flow.*

Between the variety of ways to cook with the Magic Box (*roasting, smoking, grilling, rotisserie, etc.,*) its versatility to cook at any range from cold smoking to high-heat searing (*I hate being a slave to a dial*), and the fact that I have a wide variety of smoking options (*dust, pellets, chips, or chunks*), depending on what I have available in the smoke flavors I want, the box is pretty easy going for a guy who misplaces his tongs 72 times a day!

Fun

There's just something about these roasting boxes that makes a party or get together more *entertaining.*

I've cooked for a LOT of people, in a LOT of places, and there's a camaraderie that comes with the Caja that's unique. People gather around the box, stare at the coals, sip their drinks, they drag their lawn chairs over to enjoy the heat.

We talk, we laugh, we...*interact*, more when I'm using the magic box, than with any of my other gear.

It's just more fun!

~Chef Perry
La Caja China Cooking

Chapter One
What is BBQ?

First and foremost, we have to answer the question, "What is BBQ?"

The word barbecue, when used as a noun, can refer to the cooking method, the meat cooked in this way, or to an event where this style of food is featured.

Used as an adjective, "barbecued" refers to foods cooked by this method. The term is also used as a verb for the act of cooking food in this manner. Barbecuing is usually done out-of-doors by smoking the meat over wood or charcoal. Restaurant barbecue may be cooked in large brick or metal ovens designed for that purpose.

There are numerous regional variations of barbecuing, and it is practiced in many areas of the world…we'll take a look at those a bit later.

NOTE: Despite popular marketing, the cooking apparatus used to cook with is *not* a "barbeque", it is either a GRILL, a SMOKER, or some modification, or combination of the two.

Barbecue today have taken on new meaning yet again with the emergence of competitive barbecue. Competitive barbecue competitions are held throughout the country, where people compete by cooking barbecue and having it judged by the events judges.

The constraints of what one may barbecue and the qualities that are judged vary by competition. Usually competitions are held in large open areas, where spectators are be admitted as well, and barbecue is served to all.

In the corner of the country that I live in, we have an inexplicably popular "BBQ" restaurant chain, let's call them..."Flusters", that I find myself invited to once or twice a year, by well-meaning folk who are either scared to cook for me themselves, or assume that I would favor it as a meeting place.

I...do not.

- BBQ is served FRESH

- BBQ is NOT a sauce

- Just because you put sauce ON something, doesn't make it BBQ

- BBQ is the ultimate K.I.S.S. cuisine

- BBQ was meant to be eaten OUTDOORS. If I can't toss peanut shells on the ground...

- BBQ should cause a sense of EXCITEMENT (surly, bored, teenagers "May I take your *yawn* order?" are not welcome).

A Bit of History

The English word Barbecue and cognates in other languages come from the Spanish word *barbacoa*. Etymologists believe this to be derived from *barabicu* found in the language of the Arawak people of the Caribbean and the Timucua of Florida.

The Oxford English Dictionary traces the word to Haiti and translates it as a "framework of sticks set upon posts".

Gonzalo Fernández De Oviedo y Valdés, a Spanish explorer, was the first to use the word "*barbecoa*" in 1526 "Diccionario de la Lengua Española" of the Real Academia Española.

After Columbus landed in the Americas in 1492, the Spaniards apparently found native Haitians slowly roasting meat over a grill consisting of a wooden framework resting on sticks above a fire.

The flames and smoke rose and enveloped the meat, giving it a unique flavor. The same framework was also used as protection from nocturnal animal attacks.

Traditional barbacoa involved digging a hole in the ground and placing some meat—usually a whole lamb—above a pot so the juices can be used to make a broth. It is then covered with leaves and coals, and set alight. The cooking process takes a few hours. Olaudah Equiano, an African abolitionist, described this method of roasting alligators among the Mosquito People (*Miskito people*) on his journeys to Cabo Gracias a Dios.

Linguists have suggested the word barbacoa migrated from the Caribbean and into other languages and cultures; it moved from Caribbean dialects into Spanish, then Portuguese, French, and English. According to the OED, the first recorded use of the word in English was a verb in 1661, in Edmund Hickeringill's Jamaica Viewed: "Some are slain, And their flesh forthwith Barbacu'd and eat"

(Yikes! We won't be visiting that recipe!)

The word barbecue was published in English in 1672 as a verb from the writings of John Lederer, following his travels in the North American southeast in 1669-70. The first known use of the word as a noun was in 1697 by the British buccaneer William Dampier.

In his *New Voyage Round the World*, Dampier wrote, " ... and the meat lay there all night, upon our Borbecu's, or frames of Sticks, raised about 3 foot from the Ground".

Samuel Johnson's 1756 dictionary gave the following definition:

"To Barbecue – a term for dressing a whole hog"

In the southern United States, barbecues initially involved the cooking of pork. During the 19th century, pigs were a low-maintenance food source that could be released to forage in woodlands. When food or meat supplies were low, these semi-wild pigs could then be caught and eaten.

In fact, prior to the American Civil War, Southerners ate around five pounds of pork for every pound of beef, and because of the effort to capture and cook these wild hogs, pig slaughtering became a time for celebration and the neighborhood would be invited to share in the feast. In Cajun culture, these feasts are called *boucheries* or "pig pickin's" and the traditional Southern barbecue grew out of these gatherings.

By the 19th century barbecues had become the main form of public celebration in the United States, especially in celebration of July 4.

As barbecues continued to be held through the times of U.S. expansion the traditions began to migrate with the people.

Today barbecues held in different regions of the country vary in cuisine but they all hold the same concept of cooking outside and using fire.

BBQ is NOT Grilling

Though modern accepted "barbecuing" encompasses four or five distinct types of cooking techniques, true BBQ is the technique of cooking using smoke at low temperatures (240–280 °F or 115–145 °C) with significantly longer cooking times (*several hours to overnight*). Smoking can be used to flavor, cook, and/or preserve food by exposing it to smoke.

Meat and fish are the most common smoked foods, though cheeses, vegetables, and nuts, are also smoked.

Grilling, on the other hand is done over direct, dry heat, usually a fire over 500 °F (260 °C) for a short period of time. Grilling can be done over wood, charcoal (briquettes or lump), gas, or even electricity.

The goal of grilling is (usually) to sear the surface of the food, while bringing the center to a minimum safe temperature (at least, the should be the goal, if you're a "well-done only griller...well, we'll work on that.)

La Caja China: 101

La Caja China [*Spanish* la ka'ha chee'nah] —noun - *A metal-lined roasting box in a wood frame with wheels. Charcoal is fired on a removable grate, over a solid ash-pan on top of the box, and the heat emanates through the metal lid into the enclosed space below, roasting the meat, which rests in pans or on a rack.*

The roasting box's claim to fame is its unique ability to roast a whole pig (*up to a 100 lbs, live weight*) in less than four hours.

The rack system, which is held together with 4 S-Hooks, allows you to quickly and easily flip whatever you're roasting for even cooking, and last-minute browning of a pig's skin, keeping it crispy without overcooking.

Now, La Caja China, for all the pig-related press, is one of the most versatile pieces of equipment I've used in a lifetime of cooking and barbecue. Sure, I've roasted a number of pigs in the Cuban box (*and they were delicious*) but, as a private chef and caterer, I've cooked a LOT of other stuff in and on it, too.

My team and I have prepared everything from holiday dinners like St. Patrick's Day corned beef and Thanksgiving turkeys; ethnic delights from Malaysian satays and Italian porchetta sandwiches, to Kalua pig and Moroccan lamb.

You can grill steaks, braise chickens, smoke briskets, and roast turkeys and prime-rib that rivals any restaurant, and do it all in your own backyard!

And, of course, you can roast melt-in-your-mouth whole pigs that send will send your guests into fits of gastronomical joy.

Even more importantly, you can prepare these dishes for crowds that would normally require a smoke house, a four-foot deep pit dug in your yard, multiple gas grills, and several full-size ovens...and you can do it anywhere, anytime.

The optional top-grills set into place over the coals and allow for nearly 1200 sq. inches of grilling area over the coals for the larger models (*that's a lot of burgers*) and 600 sq. inches over the Model #3. So you can grill plenty of tasty appetizers while the not-always-so-patient crowd of admirers is waiting to get their pig on.

Sometimes when I'm called on to flip burgers and grill some dogs for our youth group, I just toss the ash-pan, coal grate and these grills, along with a couple of metal sawhorses into my van, and I can grill *en masse* on a system that weighs all of around ten pounds. and sets up in 30 seconds. Nice.

The name "La Caja China" translates from Spanish into "The Chinese Box", and there are two schools of thought, regarding the name. The first is that it is a reference to the roasting boxes that Chinese railroad workers in Cuba used to cook meals.

The second is that the Cuban use of the word "China" as a slang term for something unique or inventive, was used to describe the amazing ability to cook succulent pig in such a comparatively short time.

Regardless of the name-origin, the basic idea has been used for centuries.

The current designs and their capabilities, however, are the result of years of tinkering and perfecting by Cuban pig-roasting enthusiasts.

In the South, these boxes are often referred to a "Cajun Microwaves."

La Caja China Semi-Pro

I bought my first La Caja China to feed my obsession with barbecue toys. In the years since, I have added a Model #3, and a Semi-Pro to my arsenal.

I became so enamored with them that, in 2010, I quite literally wrote the book – publishing the first (ever) roasting box cookbook, "La Caja China Cooking" with the blessing of La Caja China founder and owner, Roberto Guerra.

If you're looking for a means to roast, grill, bake, braise, smoke, or barbecue...look no further that La Caja China.

Cook for a crowd with Model 1, 2 or the awesome new "Semi Pro" model, or create perfect dinners for your own family with Model #3.

Let's face it, anyone with some basic grill-skill can cook up some burgers and dogs, a good summertime griller can throw down a tender steak, or juicy hunk of chicken, and there's always one or two backyard pit-masters in the group who can smoke a great pork shoulder or brisket.

I can tell you from experience, however...when you pull a whole hog out of La Caja China, steaming and golden, the skin crisped to salty perfection, tender, juicy white meat falling off the bone...you become a legend.

La Caja China Model #3

4 Rules for Becoming a Pit-*Master*

Pitmaster: One in charge of the pit. Someone who, not only has mastered the techniques to create great BBQ, but is proficient in using a variety of pits, or grill to do so.

While there's no one single accepted definition of the title, "Pit Master" (*in fact, they vary wildly*), I like the one above. I see someone who has "mastered" the pit, as being able to produce delicious BBQ with any number of meats, and a variety of equipment.

The proof, as they say, is in the pudding. Here are four things that I think anyone needs, to achieve the title…

1. Practice, Practice, Practice!

It can't be said enough (*though I'll stop at three times*), like anything else, the more you do it, the better you get. Chose the cut of meat you want to perfect, then keep working on it until you're doing it the best it can be done. I recommend starting with pork shoulders (*the most forgiving*) and working your way up to smaller, thinner cuts.

Experiment with varied cook times, type of smoke, rubs, marinades, brines, and the like, until you think, "Damn, it doesn't get better than that!"…then do it 10 more times.

2. Keep Notes

Repetition isn't going to take us very far, if we don't recall exactly what we did, and the results, the last time.

Date your test, and track external elements like:
- Ambient temperature
- Wind
- Type of smoke
- Amount of coals

- Time to temp (*how long, from the time the meat goes in the heat, until it reaches the target temperature.*)

You'll also want to jot down your recipe specifics:

- Cut and weight of meat
- Grade of meat, and where you bought it
- Temp prior to cooking
- Marinade recipe, rub, brine (*and time*), or injection

And, of course, your thoughts on the finished product. A 1-10 scale for taste, texture, and appearance can be helpful, too. I know some pit-master who go so far as to make before and after photos, but I'm not quite THAT anal-retentive.

3. K.I.S.S.

Keep it simple...

If you ask 10 cooks a BBQ question, you'll get 12 answers.

Don't waste your time trying every new fad or "miracle technique" you find in the comments section of your favorite BBQ blog. There are enough well-established methods to keep you busy the rest of your life! Find out what the big boys are doing (*i.e: Google*), and monkey-do. Meat, salt, and smoke is 90% of the game anyway, and some of the best BBQ in the world is made in dented old oil drums, behind wooden shacks.

As far as the "extras" (*seasonings and sauces*), learn your favorite flavor profile (*sweet, salty, sour, bitter, spicy, umami*) and spend most of your time and effort in that neighborhood.

4. Have the Right Gear

Last (*but certainly not least*) make sure you have the right tools for the job.

If you BBQ with La Caja China, you're already got a great start. After that, a high-quality meat thermometer is my most important BBQ tool. Tongs are #2 on the list...and I own a LOT of tongs (*in fact, I may be a bit obsessive on the issue*), and I use them on nearly everything. Even if you don't become a collector, like me, you'll need at least a couple of pairs, one for raw meat, and another for cooked.

When working with large cuts, never (*ever!*) use meat forks to move them around. Buy some heavy, white dish towels (*invest in bleach*), and use them to protect your hands, while carefully moving that brisket or pork shoulder from the box, to the table.

Lastly, I find an industrial food-grade spray bottle to be indispensable. Every time I lift the lid on the box, I give the meat a quick, healthy spritz of warm marinade, adding both flavor and moisture.

Which Cuts of Meat Are Best for Smoking?

Smoking is a low and slow process of cooking that uses smoke to add flavor and tenderize meats. It's an art and a favorite technique for barbecue aficionados, but what are the best types of meat to smoke?

While you may be tempted to toss your best cuts of beef and pork on the smoker, you'll find that the better choices are also the cheapest and less desirable cuts. This is great news because smoking is fun but also a bit of a challenge. Since you'll be saving money on the meat, you can enjoy the freedom of experimentation. It's one of the reasons so many people get really excited about smoking and true barbecue.

What Happens During Smoking?

Smoking usually lasts for more than 30 minutes a pound, but it can be much longer.

There are times when meat can be on the smoker for up to 20 hours. Many good, lean cuts of meat would dry out and become inedible after cooking for this long.

On the flip side, many cuts of meat that we tend to think of as "cheap" or low-quality can handle this prolonged heat. In fact, meat that is full of fat and connective tissues (collagen) is best in the smoker. The meat will actually improve and come out tender, flavorful, and downright delicious.

If you don't have patience, real barbecue is not for you. We can look to traditional barbecue meals when determining the best cuts for the smoker. The meats of barbecue are generally beef brisket, pork shoulder, and ribs. These are tough, chewy meats and generally so poor in quality that they are not good when cooked using other methods.

Barbecue takes advantage of the high fat and connective tissues in these meats and transforms them into something that's *amazing*. During the long cooking times of smoking, the fat melts and the connective tissue breaks down. This sweetens the meat and keeps it moist during smoking.

Smoking Rookies, Start Here

If you are new to smoking it's best to begin with an easy cut of meat. You cannot go wrong with a small pork shoulder roast like a Boston Butt or a picnic. Ask your butcher for these; he'll know what you're talking about.

These cuts are generally forgiving and relatively inexpensive. This makes them perfect for learning your equipment and perfecting your smoking technique. They're also good for experiments in different types of wood, temperature and time, and other factors that you can play around with. As you learn more and become comfortable with the smoking process, you can move on to larger and more difficult cuts like a brisket or ribs.

Before you know it, you'll master the art of true barbecue, because it really is an art.

Keep These Cuts out of the Smoker

In general, any cut of meat that we consider "prime or choice" should not be smoked.

It's unnecessary to spend the time and waste the wood on a meat that is already delicious and tender.

Plus, you won't taste the benefits of your efforts. Good cuts of meat like pork tenderloin, any type of steak, or a good lean roast should be reserved for other cooking methods. For outdoor cooking, grilling any of these meats is a much better option.

Chapter Two
SMOKE

Getting Started with Smoke

Smoking meat is as old as, well...smoke and meat.

Some of the best meats to slow smoke are those that aren't much good for any other cooking method.

Two of the kings of BBQ, pork shoulder and beef brisket, are real jaw-wreckers if not cooked low and slow, mature poultry is another great choice. There are plenty of meats that are great to smoke, but for starters, let's just look at the bog three...

Pork

One of the best meats to make your bones on (*so to speak*), is a good, fresh pork shoulder. These lovely hunks of pig are usually inexpensive, and very forgiving to the smoke learning curve, and experimentation. You'll want to smoke, using hickory or pecan, at around 215-225°F, for 90 minutes per pound.

Beef

In many parts of the country, beef brisket IS BBQ. Indelibly tough and bland when cooked with conventional methods, brisket magically transforms, after a long bath in smoke, into a melt-in-your mouth, sweet, savory, smoky treat.

Sliced thin (*Texas-style*) or chopped for tacos are my two favorite ways to use brisket.

One of the great things about brisket is that it's crazy-simple, with very little prep or advanced techniques required. Bring to room temp, season simply with salt, pepper, and garlic, and smoke with oak for 90 minutes per pound, at 225°F. (*See "Using the Crutch", below.*)

Chicken

Chicken, while still pretty easy, requires a little more forethought than shoulders or brisket.

First of all, whenever possible, find a plump, fresh, 3-5-pound free-range bird.

Not only do you not have to worry about what chemicals are floating around in your hen, but the taste and texture is vastly better, than some shriveled, frozen bird from the supermarket.

Like any BBQ, the secret to perfect chicken is, you guessed it...low and slow smoking! Around 235°F, for 60 minutes per pound, is what you're looking for.

For chicken, with its more delicate flavor, I like a lighter tasting wood-smoke, like apple or cherry.

Pull the chickens out of the smoke when the meat is still slightly undercooked, around 150°F, move it over the direct heat of a hot grill top, and crisp the skin on all sides.

Some folks skip this step if they're planning to shred the chicken, but I think that the crispy bits of skin really kick up the flavor of a pulled chicken sandwich, so it's worth a little extra work!

Chef's note: If you don't have enough heat left in your coals, when the chicken is done smoking, you can do this step under the broiler, as well.

What is Cold Smoking?

Cold smoking is done at low temperatures (typically between 70 and 100 degrees Fahrenheit).

Cold smoking is great for flavoring meat that will later be cooked, and is increasingly popular for flavoring cheeses. Nova Lox and Gravlax are two examples of meats that are cured prior to smoking, and then slowly cold-smoked at 70 degrees for 12-16 hours.

Dry-cured sausages, such as pepperoni and Spanish chorizo, are cold-smoked before being hung to dry for days, weeks, or months.

4 More Tips for Mastering the Curve

1. Bring to Temp

Never put cold meat in your smoker.

Meat needs to rest until it reaches room temperature.

Cooking at cold temps shocks the meat, causing it to seize up (*i.e: stay tough*).

Another benefit of room temp meat is that the pores open up, allowing better absorption of smoke, and getting the flavor deep.

You want to smoke all the way through the meat, not just the surface, or what's the point?

2. Less is More

Another key to smoking is to not *over*-smoke. Real BBQ isn't about how much smoke is billowing out of your Caja, but that your meat is getting just the right amount to maximize the flavor without getting that bitter taste that comes with over-smoking.

As far as *methods* of smoking in your La Caja China, we'll get to those in Chapter 3.

3. Use the Crutch

Wrapping large cuts of meat, like shoulders and brisket, is a step used by the pros in competition by wrapping meat in a double layer of heavy foil, halfway through the cooking process.

This helps tenderize and break down your BBQ, without drying out the outside portions, or over-smoking before it's finished.

This is especially effective with ribs. (*Just be sure to finish them quickly, over hot coals, before serving.*)

Using the crutch

4. Smoke to Temp

I've said it before, and I'm going to keep saying it…the #1 best thing you can do to create better BBQ is to get a high-quality probe thermometer.

When you cook by minutes and hours, there are too many variables that can (*and do*) effect the finished product, and there's a lot of luck involved.

Cook by temperature and you're cooking with science, which increases your likelihood of success exponentially.

Rule of thumb for Low & Slow:

- Chicken: 165°F
- Pork: 200°F
- Ribs: 195°F
- Brisket: 205°F

Make your own luck…get a thermometer.

The most important thing to remember, if you want to smoke great meat, is to smoke!

Smoke a lot, try different recipes, different techniques, different cuts…and try them often!

Know Your Smoke

Let's face it, as cooking methods go, smoking ranks pretty high on the "anyone can do this" chart. Prep is minimal, as are the number of ingredients in most recipes. The only area that many of us run into trouble is the need for patience.

We like to fiddle, to tweak, to "just take a peek", we're like children waiting, wide-eyed and anxious, staring at the ceiling for the first glimmer of dawn on Christmas morning.

Sadly, there's not much I can do to help with your impatience (*God knows, I have enough trouble trying to keep mine on a leash…*)

However, I can cover a the few OTHER basics that can help take your smoking to the next level.

Temperature Control

Most meats need to be smoked in a range between 200-225F, and to an internal temperature of between 145 and 165F (*depending on the meat*) to be safe.

"Safe", however, is just a road sign on your journey to great BBQ, which typically requires that the meat comes to at least 180F, to attain the buttery, shreddable texture that is your destination.

A digital probe thermometer is a must to know exactly when the contents of your smoker hit their sweet spot.

It's this temperature control, paired with the right amount of time, that allows the flavor of the smoke to penetrate deeply, while at the same time, breaking down the tough connective tissue in that brisket or pork shoulder (*called collagen*), transforming it into *gelatin*, which creates that amazing BBQ texture.

Your best plan is to have TWO probe thermometers, one tracking the temp of the meat, and the other monitoring the temperature inside the box, at the same level of the meat.

A halved potato, with the probe pushed through it far enough for the reader element to stick out the far side (*so it's reading the air, not the potato*) is a great way to keep that second probe reading accurately, and not touching anything that might throw of its reading.

Plus, you have a smoky delicious spud to snack on while your pig is resting!

Tips for Using a Digital Meat Thermometer

Meat thermometers are designed to measure meat doneness and temperature with great exactness and have probes long enough to be inserted into a large cut of meat before it's cooked and remain in the meat during the cooking process, and a heavy-duty heat-proof wire.

This is an ideal feature with roasting boxes, as it doesn't require the lid to be removed (*and heat to escape*) to check the temperature.

Accuracy

Your thermometer is only as useful as it is accurate! You can test food thermometers by placing them in boiling water (at least 30 seconds). If your thermometer is working properly, it should read 212°F.

It it's off, look up the manufacturer's instructions on how to calibrate it, or get a new one. An inaccurate thermometer is worse than no thermometer.

Placement

Different meats, and cuts of meats, need to be checked differently, and knowing the best place to take a reading can be tricky. With most large cuts of meat, or whole animals, you want your probe centered in the thickest part or the meat (*typically the ham on the rear leg*). Be careful not to let the probe touch any bone, as bones stay cooler than the meat around them.

For whole chickens or turkeys, insert the probe at the joint where the thigh meets the rest of the body (*this is the part that takes the longest to cook*).

For thin foods like chops or hamburgers, insert the probe sideways to about the center of the cut.

30 Second Rule

One mistake that's often made when checking temp is not allowing the probe enough time to take an accurate reading. "Instant" is a great marketing term, but don't trust it!

Most probes need 20-30 seconds, stationary, to get an accurate reading.

Cleaning & Storage

Nobody likes to use a grimy, crusty thermometer.

Not only is it unsanitary, but a mucky probe can give false temp readings, making it useless. I clean mine Immediately after each use, by scrubbing the probe of food thermometers in hot, soapy water (*after detaching it from the reader!*) and wiping down the rest of the thermometer with a damp, hot cloth to remove and grease build up.

Also, when using a probe in meat, especially poultry, you should sanitize it by dipping in boiling water or using commercial sanitizing solution. Dry all parts of the thermometer well, to prevent rust.

Finally, don't forget to turn your thermometer OFF when you're finished cooking, to preserve battery life. Finding out that your batteries are dead, when you're ready to start cooking, sucks.

Full Immersion

Next on the list, is making sure that steady (*but controlled*) amounts of clean smoke reaches all surfaces of the meat. This is why you never put the meat in a dish, or pan, as it would block smoke for reaching the bottom-side.

Instead, always set the meat directly on the grate (*or the meat rack*) to allow smoke to penetrate all sides, which allows for even cooking and smoke penetration.

Also, you always want to allow for airflow (*by removing one, or both, end rails*) so the smoke is in constant motion around the meat.

If the smoke remains stationary, it can build up creosote (*yes, that same nasty black gunk they coat railroad ties with*) giving your BBQ and unpleasant stickiness, and bitterness.

Know your Smoke II

Knowing which wood to use when smoking meats, is often the most confusing part of the process for those new to BBQ. There are a *lot* of choices, and and variations.

How do you know where to start?

I've probably tested just about every combination out there, and I tend to agree with these common suggestions:

- **Applewood:** Apple smoke has a light, fruity, flavor that imparts a slightly sweetness to the meat. Apple is great with fish, chicken, and pork ribs.
- **Cherry:** Cherry smoke is a little stronger than apple, but still considered a mild smoke. It's best for smoking cheese and poultry.
- **Alder:** Moderately mild and still slightly sweet, alder smoke is my go-to for fish (especially salmon) and seafood. My native American ancestors of the Pacific coast used alder to smoke salmon and steelhead for thousands of years, Test it with chicken and pork, too.
- **Oak:** Ah, oak...the universal smoke! Oak smoke compliments just about anything, but it's the standard for most pros, when smoking pork. Often, especially in the South, it's blended with pecan, as well.
- **Mesquite:** I don't use mesquite often, as it can often overpower the flavor of most domesticated meats. However, it's perfect for stronger (*some use the term "gamey"*) meats like venison, buffalo, and other wild game meats.

Basic rule of thumb: Heavy woods like hickory, oak, etc., for "heavy" meats (*beef, pork bison*), and light woods (*alder, fruit tree, nut-tree*) to smoke light meats like fish, fowl, or rabbit. In the end, you want a light, steady smoke that is going to compliment the flavor of the food without overpowering it. My personal favorite for whole hogs, or shoulders is half oak, half pecan.

Finally, remember...it's a *process*. Great BBQ comes from experience, and experience comes from trial and error...*lots* of trial and error.

Experiment with as many combinations of meat and smoke you can lay your hands on. Build up a catalog in your head (*or better, keep a journal*), of the various flavor profiles you create by experimenting.

Practice this enough, and you reach a point where you just...know...what smoke would best compliment any new flavor you encounter.

Remember, a "smoker" is not just a piece of equipment.

A *smoker* is someone who knows smoke!

The Wood

Ahh, smoked meat…

Is there anything better that the thick, pungent flavor of a slice of fork-tender smoked brisket, or that lovely ruby ring around the inside of a juicy chunk of pork shoulder?

(Hint: the answer is no.)

Few meats cannot be improved upon with the addition of a thick (*or thin*) blanket of aromatic, hardwood smoke.

But...to soak, or not to soak? There's the rub! (*sorry*)

Seriously, though, this is a subject I've kicked around, waffled on, and argued both sides of, for years now.

Many pit-masters insist that you need to soak wood to avoid those flash flare-ups that can occur when opening the smoker to add meat, or argue that soaked wood maintains a lower temperature, keeping it in the "smolder-zone" longer, before in ignites, and therefore giving you more bang (*or at least smoke*) for your buck.

Others preach that in order for wood to burn cleanly, it has to first be dry and "seasoned", and why bother if you're just going to allow the wood cells to soak up water?

They offer that because the temperature is kept below the point of full combustion, the burn is incomplete and the smoke and steam carry with it unburnt components, or creosote, that you really don't want on your food. (*Creosote = a gummy, tarry compound that, which often accumulates in a chimney or in your pit*)

Besides, they would say, if you soak, you just have to cook off all the steam before the wood can start smoking.

Chips or Chunks?

Chips are small pieces of wood, typically intended for quick bursts of smoke.

Even soaked in water, chips will burn up and disappear pretty quick. If you're smoking for a short period of time, or just looking for a hint of smoke flavor, you probably want to go with chips.

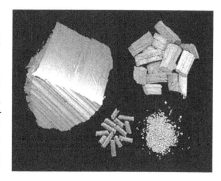

In fact, some electric and gas smokers are designed to only handle wood chips.

According to Weber, *"It's not necessary to soak wood chips before use if you're putting them in an aluminum foil pouch. When placing wood chips directly on the fire, soaking them first won't do much to keep them from bursting into flames."*

Chunks are large, irregular pieces of hardwood, typically 2-3 inches, and are best for creating a long smoke, for slow, low temperature barbecue.

If it's smokin' all day (*or all night*) you want to use chunks.

Regardless of your preference to soak or not, most of the pros seem to agree that if heavy dark smoke is billowing out every seam, hole, gap around the lid of your box...you have TOO MUCH smoke!

Starting up you'll probably smoke heavily for a short bit, but it should lessen and thin considerably. Your ultimate goal is a thin light-blue smoke that's close to invisible (*sometimes IS invisible*) but you can still smell it.

In researching this post, I found some great ideas buried in the user's comments of various articles. Here are my favorites:

- Soak both chunks/chips for a 2-3 days. Take them out of the water and put them in zip bags and freeze them. You'll always have smoking wood on hand this way, and if you forget to soak your wood, these are ready in the freezer.
- Use a 50/50 split of soaked chips and dry ...saw some guy on the food channel do that...seemed to work great.
- If you're going to soak your wood chips, soak them in wine or beer get a little more flavor going. I've even used the flavored Jack Daniels chips with great success.

In my pit, I favor the no-soak approach, mostly because I'm a big proponent of the Minion Method*.

I like to use few half-fist sized chunks of oak and hickory, buried at different depths in my charcoal pile, with a couple of chunk placed right on top.

As the pile burns down, I get an even amount of thin blue smoke, which leads to that wonderfully deep smoke ring, and great bark on my briskets and shoulders.

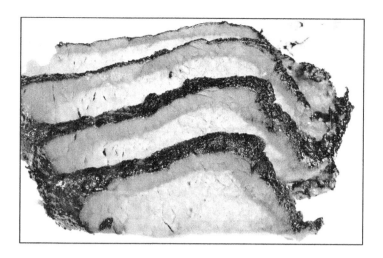

One Ring to Rule Them All..

(The Legendary Smoke Ring)

In the world of barbecue, the smoke ring is one of the most mysterious and sought-after properties of smoked meats. It is believed to show that you have done a good job and properly low and slow smoked the meat in question.

It's particularly prized in smoked brisket.

So, what is it?

A smoke ring is a pink discoloration of meat just under the surface crust (*called bark*).

It can be just a thin line of pink or a thick layer of deep crimson.

A good smoke ring is around a ¼ inch in thickness. The smoke ring is caused by nitric acid building up in the surface of the meat, absorbed from the surface. This nitric acid is formed when nitrogen dioxide from wood combustion in smoke mixes with the natural water in the meat. Basically, it is a chemical reaction between the smoke and the meat and a prized element in all types and variations of traditional barbecue.

So how to do you get the best smoke ring? Opinions vary. Generally, water-soaked wood produces more nitrogen dioxide loaded smoke than dry wood, but only by a small margin.

If you really want to make sure you get a smoke ring then cheat. Coating meat with a salt tenderizer like Morton's Tender Quick will load up the surface of the meat with nitrogen dioxide and give you a great smoke ring.

Because of the prevalence of this kind of "cheating", smoke rings are no longer taken into consideration in barbecue competitions.

Chapter Three
Smoking with La Caja China

5 Ways to add Smoke to the Magic Box

Please Note: The use of any and all of these after-market methods for adding smoke are to be done at your own risk. I'm showing you how I'VE used them, but I take <u>no responsibility</u> for individual results or any damages or injuries you may experience by using these methods yourself.

There, now that my ass is covered, let's take a look… 😉

The A-MAZE-N Smoker

With over a thousand 5-Star reviews on Amazon, it's not hard to understand why the smokers from A-Maze-N Products have become the go-to item for creating and adding great smoky flavor for home pit-masters everywhere.

Light weight, durable and portable, they produce great quality smoke for cold and hot smoking.

These little pellet burners will produce 4-5 hours of smoke at temps tested up to 275°, and are versatile enough to be used in just about any smoker or a grill.

When not in my roasting boxes, I often use mine to add a little punch in my Traeger Pro, or my little Weber grill.

At less than fifty-bucks, and with no moving parts, no electricity required, and no "special needs", the A-Maze-n products are built to perform flawlessly…and have done so for me in all sizes of La Caja China, pellet smokers, gas, and charcoal grills.

These are hands down the best "quick & easy" smoking option (*in my not-so-humble opinion*) for any roasting box.

The Differences

The A-Maze-N Smoker *AMNS* is a 5x8x2", durable and portable heavy metal mesh smoke generator, which requires no electricity and has no moving parts.

They can be used in just about any smoker or a grill. It weighs about a pound and produces very little ash.

The A-Maze-N Smoker will produce smoke for up to 11 hours on less than a pound of pellets.

This is the one I started with, and it's still my first love. As a personal chef, I take mine on every gig, along with a quart baggie of pellets, just in case.

Current Price: $34.99

www.amazenproducts.com

The **12" Tube Smoker** *AMNTS* uses the very same materials as the *AMNS* smoker, but it's in the shape of a tube.

It was designed to burn pellets and supplement smoke at higher temps, in Pellet Grills/Smokers.

This is where most pellet grills/smokers do not produce much smoke.

The AMNTS adds additional smoke at cooking temps, regardless if your pellet grill/smoker is burning pellets or not.

Just like the other smoker, the AMNTS will produce great smoke for cold smoking as well. The 12" AMNTS will burn up to 4 hours, depending on the smoker temps, type of pellets and draft inside your smoker.

Mine, kindly sent to be by Todd, worked perfectly, right out of the box.

The tube smoked consistently (*you get about 1 hour smoke per 3 inches of pellets in the tube*) for a little over 4 hours, as advertised, without having to blow on it or mess with it at all. It was literally "set it and forget it" till it burned out.

This thing smokes like an iron horse in an old western, and will make you the envy of every neighbor and dog on your block!

Current Price: $34.95
www.amazenproducts.com

Tips & Techniques

But remember...the magic box isn't just for pigs! I've done many, many pork shoulders and briskets in my caja chinas (*or "Cajun Microwaves" as some folks call them*), and I like my BBQ really smoky.

After a little trial and error, I've found that the best technique is to "cold smoke" the meat inside the Caja China (*using just the A-Maze-N smoker, and no coals on top*) for a couple of hours, refill the smoker, add the coals, and roast for the specified amount of time.

This achieves a deep smoke flavor that it incomparable to any other smoking method I've tried (*and I've tried most of them!*)

BTW, I use a small butane kitchen torch, or my larger propane camp torch to light mine. You can *never* have too many torches! 😉

Here are my tips from hundreds of hours of using my La Caja China, with both of these models of A-Maze-n smokers...

- Leave the two end rails off your La Caja China for airflow (*this creates a ¼ inch gap at either end*).

- Light the smoker with a propane torch on low, through the starter hole for 45 seconds. Do not use lighter fluid, if you need an accelerant, A-MAZE-N Products make a lighting gel that works great.

- Allow pellets to burn for 10 minutes, and then blow the flame out (this is probably the most important step in keeping the smoker smoking (*and one that many folks don't bother with...to their regret*) and set the smoker directly on top of, and centered on, the pig rack (*over the meat*). Always position your smoker above meats, never below, to avoid being extinguished by drippings.

- Keep in mind that airflow (*wind*) can shorten burn time, and increase box heat, so keep your roasting box out of direct drafts.

- Don't use a water pan in conjunction with this smoker, as the steam can kill the fire and stop the smoking process.

- Never use a smoker in an enclosed area or without proper ventilation.

- If you plan on smoking for more than 12 hours (*a packer brisket, for example*), have a second maze lit and ready to swap out, to avoid losing heat and effecting overall smoking time.

- Keep your pellets dry, dry, dry! Smoker pellets will suck moisture out of the air, and I would guesstimate that at least 95% of people who have trouble getting these smokers to light, and to keep burning, have allow their pellets to get damp.

- And finally, as I say in every post...NO PEEKING! I'll stop saying it when you stop doing it!) ;) Yes, it smells amazing, yes, you pig is becoming a glistening mahogany thing of beauty...you'll have plenty of time to "ohh and ahh" when she's finished roasting!

Oak & Pecan Pork Perfection!

Pellets

As far as what flavor of pellets to use, well...if you ask ten pit-masters what's the best wood to smoke a pig with, you'll likely get twelve different answers.

Basic rule of thumb: heavy woods like hickory, oak, etc., for "heavy" meats (beef, pork bison), and light woods (alder, fruit tree, nut-tree) to smoke light meats like fish, fowl, or rabbit.

In the end, you want a light, steady smoke that is going to compliment the flavor of the food without overpowering it. My personal favorite for whole hogs, or shoulders is half oak, half pecan pellets. For brisket, I use an oak/mesquite blend.

To see it in action, you can view my YouTube video, **www.cajachinavideos.com**

How Long Can I Smoke?

- Once lit, the A-Maze-N Smoker Maze will smoke up to 12 hours on 1 lb. of pellets!

- Each row of the Maze will smoke for approximately 2-3 hours, at 225F *(no coals), making it perfect for low and slow pulled-pork bbq.

- Airflow (wind) can shorten burn time, so keep the cooker out of direct drafts.

- The 6" Tube Smoker will smoke for approximately 2 hours on 1/2 lb. of pellets. The 12" Tube Smoker will smoke for approximately 4 hours on 3/4 lb. of pellets

- As with the Maze Smoker, airflow (wind) can shorten burn time, so keep the cooker out of direct drafts.

3 Steps to Smokey Goodness

1. Fill the A-Maze-N Smoker properly with approximately 1lb of pellets, or 1" from the top on the tube smokers.

2. Light the smoker with a propane torch on low, through the starter hole for 45 seconds.

3. Smoke - allow pellets to burn for 10 minutes, and then blow the flame out.

Place in an area of your grill that has good ventilation.

The Smoke Pistol

The Smoker Pistol is an electric smoke generator that mounts to the outside of the box and blows in smoke from a single-use cartridge (*you purchase the cartridges in multiples*).

Given average temps and conditions, the Smoker Pistol will provide continuous controllable smoke for up to 4 hours on a single cartridge

The Smoke Pistols do exactly what their made to do – produce smoke.

However, the requirement of an electrical plug in is problematic for me, as I find myself cooking in places that have no power on a fairly regular basis. Also, and honestly, the smoke pistol can be bit of a learning curve (*or maybe you just need be smarter than me...*)

That said, there are many thousands of folks out their happily smoking up delicious meals with both.

Current Price: $69.95

Smoker Boxes

You can always go old-school and add a wood-chip smoker box.

Personally, I'm not a fan. Unless given a LOT of airflow, they tend to fizzle out quickly, and given ENOUGH air flow, they burn up fast and hot.

Yes, they're cheap…but I haven't found them to be worth the ten bucks.

'Nuff said.

Off Set Fireboxes

From a coolness factor alone, the off-set fire box is hard to beat. With it you can really claim old-school status by smoking with split logs and wood chunks.

Despite its name, the offset isn't used to produce heat (*that still comes from up top*). Instead, you add a small number of burning coals to the barrel, and place your wood on top.

The offset can produce a LOT of smoke.

In fact, until you get dialed in on using one, there's a real risk of over-smoking.

The downside, at least for me, is that it requires some engineering chops to install safely.

You can purchase fireboxes, like the one above, from hardware sites like Home Depot, Lowes, and even Walmart for around $70.

I suggest buying the style that comes with legs, and assembling so that the firebox rests on the ground, to lessen the danger of that extra weight warping, or damaging the ply-wood end wall of the box.

However, these units do not include the brackets, heat resistant gaskets, piping, or any other materials required to actually attach it to the box.

Special saw blades may also be required to cut the proper whole in the side on the box (*as low as possible, without endangering the integrity of the box wall.*)

These items will likely add up to more than the cost of the firebox itself.

Side Note: La Caja China sent me a prototype, years ago, of the box above with an attached offset firebox.

Unfortunately, at the time of this writing, they have not released this line commercially, and I don't hold out much hope that they will soon, or ever.

Also, you want to have enough pipe to allow for some space between the firebox and the wall of the Caja, to make sure wood surface of your roasting box doesn't over heat. I make sure to add my coals to the near side of the firebox, as well (opposite the attachment) for the same reason.

IF you have the mechanical and carpentry skills to do all of this, without ruining your roasting box, then this is a great option for adding smoke.

The Controlled Burn

A great way to improve heat control in an off-set firebox, is with a "controlled burn" (*shown above*), setting up a single, double, or triple deep row of coals, with wood chunks positioned along the top.

By lighting just one end or the row, the coals will burn slowly, each igniting the next, and only burning the wood on top of the coals that are lit.

The more layers of coals, the greater the heat produced (*I typically don't do more that two layer, and more often just one*).

This method (*which also works great in a Weber kettle grill, btw*) may seem a little O.C.D. but it can produce hours of light smoke, while adding as little, or as much heat as your recipe calls for.

It's really a great method.

David Lantz's D.I.Y. Off-Set Smoker

Fellow Caja-Master David M. Lantz, posted this over on the La Caja China Owners Group (*Facebook*), and kindly gave me the okay to share.

He MacGyvered this beauty using an A-MAZE-N smoker, a table top grill, some tubing and fittings, and used it to smoke 18 racks of ribs inside his magic box.

God Bless America, Baby!

The copper tube disconnects, and David puts a brass cap on the brass fitting when he's not using the Caja China for smoking. Total cost was about $60.00 in parts he purchased at Lowe's.

Prepping the Grill Box

(As told by David)

I used the "Original Outdoor Cooker, tabletop gas grill" which as $25 at Lowe's. When you assemble it, remember that you don't need burner or stuff for burner.

Also, you'll want to trim down grill grate to fit lower in the bottom of the grill, as a shelf for the A-MAZE-N smoker.

Grill has vent holes that you can cover with a few layers of aluminum tape.

Tape all of the side holes but NOT THE BOTTOM HOLES! Air will vent up through the bottom holes and push your smoke through the tube and into the roasting box.

Parts & Assembly

* 3" articulating galvanized furnace vent, comes out the top of the grill. Cut a 3" hole in grill lid, cut tabs on pipe, pop rivet in place and tape with aluminum duct tape.

* 3" flexible aluminum dryer duct, insert onto vent tube and tape.

* 3" x 1 ½" PVC reducer. Put the dryer vent tube end inside and tape with aluminum tape.
* 1 short piece of 1 ½" PVC SCHED 40 pipe. Push this inside reducer, but do not glue, or tape!
* 1 ½ in. PVC SCHED 40 coupling. Push on PVC pipe, tape
* 1 ½" PVC SCHED 40 bushing. Push into PVC coupling and tape.

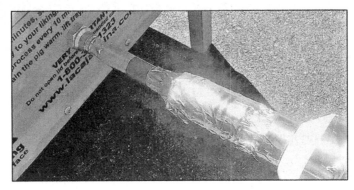

Working from the pig box out:

* 1" x 3/4" FIP brass coupling.
* 1" MIP x 3/4 FIP brass bushing, bushing and coupling screw together through a hole drilled into your box. I used a 1 1/8" spade bit but needed to open it a bit with a Dremel tool to get the bushing/coupler through. There will be only few threads to screw them together but it will tighten and stay. Inside should be nearly flush except for hex head, outside will receive below –
* 3/4" MIP both ends by 2" long brass nipple, this should screw into the brass fitting outside the box.
* 3/4" brass cap for when you are not smoking.
* 1" x 6" L copper tubing. When you want to smoke, thread the copper tubing onto the brass nipple (just enough to get it on), and seal with aluminum tape, then push the PVC bushing on to the copper tube and tape that as well.

You now have a closed system.

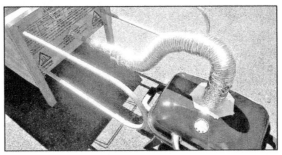

Notes:

1) When you cut the tabs on the chimney pipe, cut them all the way around and evenly. You only need to rivet or screw 4 or 5 of the tabs.

2) Remember to take the La Caja China end rail off the end opposite the pipe to create a draw on the smoke.

3) Start the smoker before you put the bushing over the copper pipe and tape it. You made need to hold the flexible aluminum dryer tube straight up to get the smoke drawing but as soon as the smoke comes out the bushing you can connect it to the copper pipe.

Note: A-MAZE-N was started from both ends, so I got about a 3 hour burn time.

Normally 6 hours when lit from one end.

When done smoking, remove tape from both side of copper tube and separate.

Then, just replace brass end cap and pig box will hold heat for roasting.

If like me, you have no idea what half of this stuff is, do what I did…just make a list, go to Lowes, and find someone wearing an apron. ~Chef Perry

Check out David's video on YouTube, here: **https://bit.ly/2NyC9o6**

Chapter Four
Techniques

Injecting

Over the last 15 years (*and a hundred-plus hogs*), I have test every possible technique I could find for adding complimentary flavors to my pigs before roasting or smoking.

Some worked, some didn't, but the two most effective methods I've found, producing the best flavors and textures, are immersion marinating and injecting.

Of the two, I vastly prefer to inject, and I'll tell you why:

1. Injecting gets your flavorings to the center of the meat immediately, as opposed to marinating, which can poorly effect the texture of outer layers of the meat, by the time the marinade has penetrated to the to the middle of the hams and shoulders.

2. It's cheaper. 2-3 quarts of injection will flavor a whole pig, with some left over for basting and mixing.

   When a marinade, you need several GALLONS to fully submerge your hog (and a leak-proof container to hold it all.

3. Marinating works, there's no question about that, but by fully submerging your pig, the entire skin is going to become completely saturated with liquid, making it nearly impossible to get that skin crispy at the end of your roast.

And, let's face it folks...that saltly, crunchy skin is the best part! (*Maybe it's just me...*) 😉

Injecting Tips

If you're using any herbs or spices in your injection that won't dissolve (*salt is fine*), be sure to strain ALL of the liquid you intend to inject through a superfine mesh, or cheesecloth, before filling your injecting syringe. Constantly having to unplug the needle when you have an entire pig to inject is a pain in the butt.

Inject 24 hours before you plan to roast. This gives your injection time to evenly permeate throughout the pig.

Inject marinade into pig every 2-3 inches, aiming for the center (top to bottom) of the portion you're injecting. Brush interior of pig with ½ of remaining marinade.

After injecting your pig or shoulder, apply a salt rub all over the meat, use Kosher salt or coarse sea salt.

Reserve remaining marinade to sprinkle over chopped pork before serving.

BASIC INJECTION:

- *32oz Apple Juice*   *32oz Water*
- *1/2 cup fine sea salt*   *1/2 cup brown Sugar*
- *1/2 cup dark molasses*   *1/2 cup apple cider vinegar*
- *1 TBS Worcestershire sauce* *1 TBS soy sauce*

Combine all ingredients and simmer for 15-20 minutes. Allow to rest and cool to room temp.

Inject every couple of inches, especially in the shoulders and hams, and rest the pig for 24 hours.

Keep remaining marinade warm and apply to pig before you close La Caja China, when you flip the pig, and again when the pig is done cooking.

(Use these same directions for the following recipes, as well)

CUBAN MOJO

This classic Cuban seasoning sauce makes a flavorful marinade for meats and poultry. Traditionally this is made with sour oranges, cumin, and lots of garlic.

With larger cuts (*pork shoulder, or whole pig & lamb*) it can be injected into the meat 12-24 hours before cooking.

- *2 C sour orange juice*   *1 Tbs oregano*
- *1 Tbs bay leaves*   *1 whole garlic bulb*
- *2 tsp cumin*   *¼ cup salt*
- *2 cups of water*

Peel and mash the garlic cloves. Mix all the ingredients and let it sit for a minimum of one hour. You can replace the sour orange juice with the following mix: 1 ¾ orange juice, ¼ cup lemon juice.

SOUTHERN BBQ

This recipe is for the whole hog, but really, it can be used for all types of pork.

If you're preparing smaller cuts of pork, simply scale back the quantities.

Use as a marinade, and injection, a mop, and finally, as a wash on the finished meat, just before serving.

- *1 qt. apple juice* *1 qt. apple cider vinegar*
- *¼ C fine sea salt* *¼ C garlic powder*
- *¼ C smoked paprika* *1 C light oil*
- *1 tsp black pepper* *1 tsp cayenne pepper*

Combine all ingredients and simmer for 15-20 minutes.

Inject every couple of inches, especially in the shoulders and hams, and rest the pig for 24 hours.

For a more traditional "Eastern" North Carolina mop, use only the apple juice, vinegar, salt, and cayenne. For South Carolina, add 1 cup prepared mustard to that.

Marinades

What Makes a Great Marinade?

One of the simplest ways to flavor food is to marinate it. That is, treat it like a sponge.

Basically, you mix up a bunch of ingredients in liquid, and soak the meat in it, allowing the meat to absorb the favors it's submerged in.

Salt, sun, oils, spices, and marinades all started out as ways to preserve meat in pre-refrigeration societies, and they discovered that they were a great was to improve the flavor of the meat, as well. Worcestershire sauce is one of the results of those early attempts to preserve foods.

Marinades typically consist of a fat, an acid, an oil, and spices, and works on all kinds of meat, as well as fish, tofu and vegetables. You can order classic mixes like Cuban Adobo, or make up your own (*more on that in my next post…*)

Fats

Flavored oils can add a lot of flavor to you meat while, at the same time, making for a juicer end product.

If you prefer to NOT add flavor, but still want added moistness, consider using Grapeseed oil, which is both flavorless and high a very high smoke point.

Some of my flavorful favorites are olive, peanut, truffle, sesame, walnut, or chili oil. I often use coconut milk, buttermilk, or yogurt, as well.

Acids

(Vinegars, lemon juice, wine, beer, spirits, or yogurt)

The acidic ingredient softens the meat, chemically altering the muscle fibers, and allowing it to absorb the flavors of the sauce. Since acids can be vinegar, wine, beer, lemon juice, lime juice, etc., they can also greatly enhance on the flavor.

Tenderization can also be caused by enzymes found in some fruits and vegetables.

Just like with acids, the muscle fibers are broken down by the fruit and veggie enzymes, too.

These enzymes are in foods such as raw onion, fresh ginger, pineapple, and green papaya. Another even more powerful form of "tenderization" comes from fermented dairy foods like yogurt and buttermilk.

The bacteria in these milk products, with their digestive qualities, breaks down the muscle fibers, and meat seems to stay moister when these are used.

Seasonings

Fresh or dried herbs, ground spices, and chilies, shallots, garlic, ginger, citrus zest; condiments such as mustard, ketchup, or fish sauce. For your oil base, try olive, peanut, truffle, sesame, walnut, or chile oil.

You can also use milk, coconut milk, buttermilk, or yogurt. For acids, experiment with vinegars, citrus juice, and yogurt. Again, you can get premixed seasoning for specific flavor combinations, as well.

Alcohol - As well as being an acid, alcoholic products like wine, beer, and spirits as work to add a great flavor punch to he finished product. Two current favorites for BBQ and grilling are bourbon and tequila (*my favorite...sometime I even use it on the meat...*)

Things like soy sauce Worstershire sauce, miso, and fish sauce make great kickers, as well.

Ratios

As far as ratios, that's up to you, but a good rule of thumb is…

"Easy as 1, 2, 3"

1 part acid + 2 seasonings, + 3 parts fat or oil + = 1 great marinade!

Tips:

- Save time by planning your marinating time in advance, like beginning the night before, or before you leave for work in the morning.
- Mom always told us we should throw out the rest of the marinade when done.
  This, as it turns out, is not always true.
  If you bring your marinade to a continuous boil for at least 60 seconds, it's perfectly safe and can make an excellent base for sauce or glazes.
- As handy as those disposable aluminum pans are, NEVER use them to marinade, as a chemical reaction can spoil the food.

- Always marinate in the refrigerator, and remove the meat from the brine before bringing it to room temp. This significantly reduces the onset of bacteria.

In all, marinade is probably the most effective and simple ways to add a ton of flavor and tenderness to what might be a cheap or tough cut of meat.

So, we've looked at how marinades were developed, the components (*fat, acid, and seasoning*) that make up a basic marinade, and the reason why marinating is a great option for skinless BBQ meats.

Now, let's delve a little deeper and talk about how you can build on that foundation to create your own unique and amazing marinades!

We'll start from a very basic marinade:

- *3/4 cup each olive oil*   *1/4 cup cider vinegar*
- *juice of 1 lemon*   *2 cloves chopped garlic*
- *1/4 teaspoon each salt and pepper.*   *1/4 c Tequila*

From that you can customize your marinade to suit the dish:

Tex-Mex: 1/4 cup chopped fresh cilantro, 2 tsp cumin and 1 tsp hot pepper sauce. Swap lemon juice with juice and zest of 1 lime.

Mediterranean: Add 1/2 cup (*total*) chopped herbs…I like parsley, oregano, basil, and a couple of splashes of Worcestershire sauce. Replace the cider vinegar with balsamic.

Asian: Add two star anise pods, and a stick of cinnamon. Replace cider vinegar with rice vinegar, and swap out the salt 2 tablespoons pure soy sauce. Stir in 1/4 cup finely chopped scallions.

Whisk all of the ingredients together and add the meat in a glass or non-aluminum bowl.

As all surfaces of the meat must come in contact with the marinade, I've found I get the best results by vacuum-packing the meat in bags.

This method requires less marinade, as well.

How long to Marinade

How long you should marinate depends on what you're marinating. Here are a few general pointers, keeping in mind that things like thickness, density, and fat/protein rations all play a factor as well.

Small pieces of fish in lime juice at room temperature would only need a few minutes to marinate.

A 10-pound beef brisket in soy sauce in the refrigerator might need to marinate overnight or longer.

Chicken - You can marinate chicken whole or in parts, but poking a few holes in the skin first will held the marinade get down deep.

Personally, I prefer to brine whole birds (*chickens and turkeys*) and marinate cut pieces.

Typically, you don't need to marinate chicken longer than two hours for the meat to soak up the flavor, but USDA guidelines allow for up to two days.

I like to marinade boneless, skinless chicken thighs for 24 hours in my favorite teriyaki sauce, before grilling it with some veggies and serving over rice.

However, keep in mind that the more acid you have in your recipe, the less time you want to marinade, as it can toughen the meat if left in too long.

Beef/Lamb - Tough cuts like flank, hanger, skirt, sirloin, and, of course, brisket, can really improve in both texture and flavor by marinating. Usually you'll want to marinate these cuts for up to 24 hours.

For high end steaks, like porterhouse or rib-eye, I wouldn't advise marinating, as it will actually break down the marbling, and make them tougher.

Pork - Thin cuts like pork chops and medallions can be marinated for as little as 1/2 hour.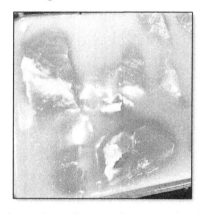

For thicker cut pork chops and steaks, marinate for 2-4 hours.

When marinating whole shoulders, poke a few 1 inch incisions all over the shoulder to let the marinade really seep in.

Make sure you don't marinate for more than 24 hours, though; your meat will break down too much and become mushy.

Keep in mind that boneless shoulders are going to have less flavor after roasting than bone in, so marinate them longer.

Whole Pigs

You can marinate whole pigs (*I have*), but I usually don't recommend it for two reasons.

First, it takes a LOT of marinade to cover a whole pig, and that can get spendy.

Second, you don't want to saturate all that lovely skin with liquid, as it won't crisp and, let's face it, crispy skin is the whole point!

If you want to get next-level flavor into a whole pig with a brine or Mojo marinade, go with an injector, and keep that skin dry!

Fish - Most fish/shellfish should really only marinade for 30 minutes and not more than an hour; after that you begin to get a "ceviche effect, as the fish begins to "cook" in the acids and gets mushy.

GREAT for eating raw, but not so good if you're planning on cooking it.

Also, avoid heavy flavors in your marinade, especially with milder, lighter fleshed product.

The whole point is to enjoy the taste of the fish, right?

RUBS

What is a Rub?

A Rub is a spice and/or herb blend that's used to coat meats prior to cooking.

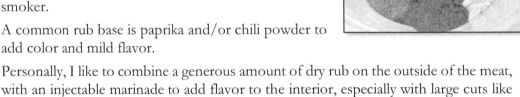

Rubs can be completely dry or can incorporate some liquids. This is called a wet rub or paste. Rubs are typically used in barbecue and grilling because they stick to the meat whether it's on a gas grill or in a smoker.

A common rub base is paprika and/or chili powder to add color and mild flavor.

Personally, I like to combine a generous amount of dry rub on the outside of the meat, with an injectable marinade to add flavor to the interior, especially with large cuts like pork shoulders.

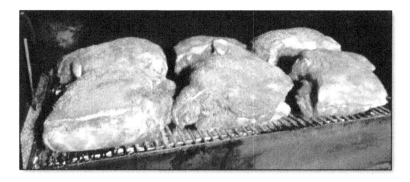

Mixing Your Own Rub

Homemade dry rubs are cheap, simple to make, and usually taste better than store-bought varieties, plus they can be easily tailored to your personal tastes or dietary restrictions.

Once you nail down the basics, you can create an endless variety of dry rubs.

A good dry rub should include five elements: A base, a salty element, a sweet element, a spicy element, and a signature element.

Base: *I like smoked paprika for a solid rub base, but many folks use a hot or sweet paprika as well. You can customize your paprika base by adding chili powder or cumin.*

Salty: This would be salt. Avoid iodized table salt in your rub (in fact, avoid that stuff in anything you plan to eat…) common options are Kosher or sea salt (coarse or medium), seasoned salt, hickory or smoked salt, or for pastes and wet rubs, you can try soy sauce or Thai fish sauce for your salt element.

Sweet: Again, an almost endless list of options: white or brown sugar, honey, molasses, or maple syrup (wet), ginger, cinnamon, etc.

Spicy: Black, white, and red ground peppers, red pepper flake, or for serious spice, try a little (*a little!*) ghost pepper powder.

Signature: Finally, make it your own with a dash or two of something you like, spices like coriander, garlic powder, onion powder, oregano, mustard, rosemary, and thyme.

Even garam masala or curry power…anything goes!

Make it a cup at a time, and tweak your recipe until it's perfect!

My "secret" pork shoulder rub…

- *¼ C smoked paprika*
- *¼ C light brown sugar*
- *2 Tbs onion powder*
- *2 Tbs coarse black pepper*
- *1 tsp cayenne powder*

¼ C coarse sea salt
2 Tbs garlic powder
2 Tbs Italian seasonings
1 Tbs hickory salt

Apply the rub generously to the inside of a butterflied pork shoulder, roll it, tie it, and apply more rub to the outside. You MUST allow the rubbed shoulder to rest in the fridge at least overnight so that the rub will help form that wonderful "bark" while roasting.

Finally, after it's done cooking and you've pulled, chopped, or shredded the meat, give it one last sprinkle for an intense, spicy flavor.

Temp Tips

Again, the biggest favor you can do yourself is to pick up a probe thermometer.

The ability to check the meat temp, without opening the box, is *vital*. I like to cook my pork shoulders to an internal temp of 195 for pulling or shredding.

Then I wrap it in heavy foil, wrap *that* in a towel, and let the whole think rest in a dry cooler for at least an hour, before shredding.

Another important temp control method is to make sure that you clean the ashes out from under the coal grate every couple of hours.

Ash is a great insulator and an inch-thick layer can easily keep your Caja China 30-50 degrees below your goal temp (225-250d).

The catch-22 is that you need to get rid of the ashes, but you want to avoid removing the ash pan, if at all possible.

I do this by lifting the coal grate and turning it sideways across one end of the ash pan, then I use a large metal dust pan (square edge) and scoop out as much ash as possible. Then I slide the coal grate to the other end, and remove the rest of the ashes the same way.

You see the temp jump 30-50 degrees when you do this.

I've found that the standard Weber charcoal chimney holds almost exactly 5lbs of coals, so I usually start with three of these and, yes, the temp will spike quite high at first.

This is why I'll often tent my shoulders (loosely) with foil during the first part of cooking. I've also found that if I use even a little less coal (say, 10lbs) the roaster will not maintain cooking temp. It seems that there is a "critical mass" temp that the Caja China need to reach to cook correctly. This is also why it's so important to not lift the lid until you reach finished temp.

Personally, I never use lump coal on La Caja China. Lump tends to burn hotter and faster, which is what I'm trying to avoid with the roaster, lol.

I only use Kingsford charcoal, as I've found it to have a uniform and reliable heat and burn time from one bag to the next.

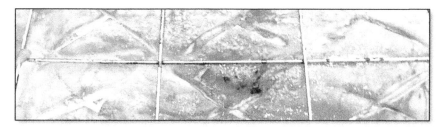

Super Crispy Skin on Whole Roast Pig

One of the questions I'm asked most often is how to achieve that super crispy "pig candy" skin when roasting a pig in La Caja China.

First of all, just following the directions on the box itself is great start, and will get you a yummy crisp skin. For that "potato-chip" crisp that makes Cuban and Fillipino *lechón* so amazing, however, I suggest a couple of things above and beyond the typical recipe. The first two steps can be used with any "whole hog" cooking method, while the third is specific to your roasting box.

The fact is, the dryer skin is when you start cooking, the crisper is will turn out. That lovely crunchy skin on *Peking Duck* comes from air-drying the duck's skin prior to cooking.

Similarly, there are a couple of things you can to to get super-crunch results with your pig.

The night before roasting, pat the entire pig down with paper towels to remove excess moisture. Then, rub the skin generously with a salt-heavy rub, or straight sea salt.

I recommend a fine grind, as it will adhere better.

Second, ss you bring the pig to room temp (*which is a must*), set up a fan – or, preferably, two – pointed at the uncovered pig, to help to help "air-dry" the skin as much as possible.

If your fan(s) can't cover the whole carcass at one time, move them around every 30 minutes or so. (*Yes, I know these are ducks…but you get the idea!*)

Btw, if you want *that* recipe, visit the website and search for *"Peking Duck ala La Cajita China"*)

Third, when you flip your pig to brown the skin for the last 30 minutes or so, pat the skin down again with paper towels, give it another sprinkle of salt, and (*most important*) set the coal tray back on at a slight angle so that there are gaps on both sides of the box.

This will allow any excess moisture cooking out of the skin to escape the box, instead of being contained and "steaming" the skin.

Watch your pig carefully at this point, as a dry skin will brown (*and burn*) much faster than one with a high moisture content.

A Word about Mops

Barbecue "Mops" or basting sauces, are typically thin, vinegar based liquids that are applied to meats during the slow cooking process of traditional barbecue, to keep the meat moist and add flavor. Tomato juice, vinegar, apple cider, beer, citrus juices, or a combination of the above, are typical ingredients.

Mops have been used for almost as long as meat has been cooked over fire. In the old, open-air pits, moisture would steam off during the long hours of slow cooking over red-hot coals. Mopping helped the meat retain its moistures and stay tender, instead of becoming giant slabs of jerky.

History

To keep all that meat moist, he mopped it with a thinned sauce…using a real mop.

Hence the barbeque term, "mop."

Legend has it that President Johnson loved his barbeque, and often called upon his favorite pit-master to cook for hundreds of guests. The meal would be cooked on a forty square-foot open air fire pit. The cook would cover every inch of this in ribs, briskets, halved pigs, and just about any other meat he could think of.

Today you can buy a miniature tool that looks like a kitchen mop to mop your meat. the cotton fibers hold the thin mop sauce and make it easy to dash large amounts on at once.

It's preferable to a basting brush, as it's less likely to wipe off seasoning that are already on the meat.

Roasting or smoking inside La Caja China, moisture retention isn't as critical of an issue as it is with open pits, but if you're going to pull off the top to dump the ashes, or flip a pig anyway, mopping will add even more layers of flavor and juiciness to the meat.

Chef Perry's Pig Pickin' Mop

This recipe is for the whole hog, but in reality it can be used for all types of pork. If you're preparing smaller cuts of pork, simply scale back the quantities. Use as a marinade, and injection, a mop, and finally, as a wash on the finished meat, just before serving.

I like to add the mayo, which doesn't really add any flavor, but because it thickens the mop slightly, allowing it to rest on the meat longer, and be absorbed more than thinner mops that quickly run off the "high points", as well as adding a little fat.

- *1 qt. apple juice*   *1 qt. apple cider vinegar*
- *2 cups real mayonnaise*   *¼ C fine sea salt*
- *¼ C garlic powder*   *¼ C smoked paprika*
- *1 C light oil*   *1 tsp black pepper*
- *1 tsp cayenne pepper*

Combine all and cook at a low simmer for 15-20 minutes. Keep warm and apply when you flip the pig (rib side), and again when the pig is done cooking (skin side).

Beef Rib Mop

- *3/4 C brown sugar*   *1/2 C bottled barbecue sauce*
- *1/2 C ketchup*   *1/2 C cider vinegar*
- *1/2 C Worcestershire sauce*   *1 C water*
- *1 Tbs salt*   *1 Tbs chili powder -- optional*
- *1 Tbs paprika*

This mop is great for brisket, as well. Keep warm and apply to ribs before you close La Caja China, when you flip the ribs, and again when the ribs are done cooking.

Recipes

Beef & Lamb

Humans have been eating beef since prehistoric times, and for good reason.

Pound for pound, beef is one of the best sources of high-quality protein and nutrients. It's also the third most widely eaten meat in the world, accounting for about 25% of modern meat production, after pork and poultry .

I love beef. It's such a straightforward and simple food to cook. Though you can get fancy with it, if you want to, all you really need is a little salt and heat to create the most delicious foods on the planet. Loaded with health-promoting amino acids, and it's one of the single biggest sources of protein in the human diet.

How Much to Serve

I recommend 8oz (½ lb) per "average" person, or ¾ lb (12 oz) for big and lovers of leftovers.

Definitions

Grass Fed

"Grass fed" beef refers to cattle which were allowed to graze for their own fresh forage, possibly supplemented with some alfalfa during the winter, providing the closest approximation to the animal's natural diet.

Grains, which are much higher in calories, allows you to grow cows much faster and cheaper, but lacks many key nutrients like Omega-3s and B vitamins.

Grass feeding takes longer, which reflects in more expensive beef, but the result is steaks and roasts that are leaner, healthier, and have a much richer, beefier flavor.

Organic

Organic products, including meat animals, must be produced and raised without synthetic pesticides, fertilizers, or GMOs and managed using conservation and sustainability techniques. Organic beef is produced in such a way that ensures both the health and welfare of the animals. allowing for no antibiotics or added growth hormones, requiring organic feed and year-round access to the outdoors. From an eating standpoint, happy and healthy animals taste better.

Aging

Dry aged beef is hung in humidity-controlled coolers, usually for at least 30 days, and often much more. As the meat ages, moisture escapes and the beef shrinks in size (up to 15%), concentrating its flavor, and softening the meat. The result is an extraordinarily rich flavor and melt-in-your-mouth texture. Dry aging also requires additional trimming before cooking, sometimes up to 50%, all of which helps to explain the very high price-tag on dry-aged beef.

Wet aging is done by sealing the meat in a plastic bag, and aging in a refrigerated room. 3 weeks is the minimum aging required for any beef, and natural (grass fed) requires more than 6 weeks to break-down and tenderize.

The truth is, many times you'll find that that supermarket steak is unusually tough simply because it *hasn't* aged long enough. Depending on the cut of beef, BBQ cook times can take up to 20 hours, with temperatures seldom rising about 250F. This slow cooking process breaks down the fibers and collagen that make these cuts of beef tough, and transforms them into gelatin, creating an unctuous, buttery tenderness, and give the smoke time to really soak in, and add its unique flavor to your beef.

Ribeye Roast

This is the classic Christmas, or Sunday roast in many parts of the world. The fine texture and generous marbling make ribeye roast a delicious and forgiving cut.

Sirloin Tip Roast

A lean, boneless cut, the sirloin tip roast is a favorite for thin-sliced beef recipes like pit-beef, French dip, and cheese-steak.

Cook and slice it as thinly as possible (*chilling it first, helps*) for some of the best beef you'll ever taste! Smoke to 140°F for medium rare; 150°F for medium and let rest at least 20 minutes.

If you're going to chill it, before slicing, allow the roast to rest at least an hour, slice in half, and wrap each half tightly in plastic wrap, before placing them in the refrigerator overnight. Moving the roast to the freezer for 15-20 minutes before slicing, can make it even easier.

Beef on a Budget

In my not-so-humble opinion, one of the great unsung cuts from the noble cow is the chuck roast.

The chuck contains a lot of connective tissue, including collagen, which partially melts during cooking. Meat from the chuck is usually used for stewing, slow cooking, braising, or pot roasting. It is particularly popular for use as ground beef, due to its richness of flavor and balance of meat and fat.

More importantly, it's cheap, it's plentiful, and it eats like an old boot…unless you know a couple of tricks to make a moist, buttery, "mock flank" out of it.

Which I do. The key to taming this muscle cut lies in two techniques:

    1. A collagen-busting, vinegar-based marinade. *(A pineapple juice marinade would work equally well.)*

    2. Taking <u>as long as possible</u> to bring the meat to 145 degrees.

I also like to use an herb/spice butter for serving, to help add moisture, and an instant-read thermometer, so I don't *(ever, ever, ever)* have to cut into meat to check for doneness, which allows valuable juices to escape.

Mock Flank Steak

- 2 – 4 lbs chuck roast, cut 2" thick
- 1 Tbs onion powder
- 1 tsp oregano

2 Tbs fresh garlic, minced
1 Tbs celery salt
1-2 cups of Italian dressing

Steak butter

- 1/4 lb unsalted butter
- 1 Tbs fresh shallots, minced
- 1/2 Tbs coarse black pepper

2 Tbs seasoned salt
1 Tbs smoked paprika

Marinade meat 8-10 hours in an oil and vinegar based Italian or vinaigrette dressing, remove from marinade, and blot dry.

Mix all spices and rub both sides of roast, then let stand at room temperature for 1 hour to air dry (preferably on a rack). You want that exterior DRY...that's the key to that delicious brown, crusty exterior.

Warm butter and add seasoned salt, shallots, paprika, and pepper, blending well.

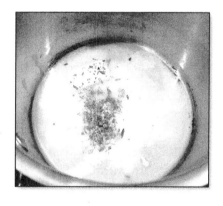

Cool slightly until spreadable. (*You can put it in the fridge to cool, but be sure to stir it every few minutes.*)

Spread a double layer of coals under one section of your coal grate, and a single layer next to it. Lightly oil the top grate. Place meat on hot side of the grill, fat side up, and grill five minutes per side.

Move roast to inside the box. You can place a drip pan under it to catch the drips which will make a great gravy later.

Smoke, with oak or mesquite, for about 1 hour or until it reaches your desired doneness (145F).

Remove roasts from the Caja China, flip, smear with remaining steak-butter, tent loosely with foil, and allow to rest 15-20 minutes to before cutting in 1/8" slices across the grain.

Serve immediately.

Brisket

I've made many, many slow-smoked briskets in my roasting boxes and when you get it right...there's nothing better.

This chest muscle, packed with tough-as-tires collagen, needs a long cook with very low heat (225F-ish) to transform that hard tissue into soft, unctuous gelatin.

And it's worth every minute!

Preparing

If you have a frozen brisket, let it thaw in the refrigerator for 2 days to defrost thoroughly. Two hours before you plan to begin cooking, take the brisket from the refrigerator. Remove the plastic packaging, rinse brisket well with cool water, and pat dry.

Resting

At a minimum, place the brisket on a rimmed baking pan, cover loosely with foil, and let rest 30 minutes before slicing. 60-90 minutes is better.

Brisket Yield

When you take into account the trimming of the brisket before and after cooking, plus the shrinkage that occurs during cooking, don't be surprised if you end up with a 50% yield of edible meat from a whole, untrimmed brisket.

That means 6 pounds of edible meat from a 12 pound brisket.

Depending on the brisket and the internal temp you cook it to, it may be as low as 40% or as high as 60%.

If you're cooking brisket for a party, figure 4-5 ounces of meat per sandwich or 6 ounces of sliced meat on a plate (8 ounces for hearty eaters).

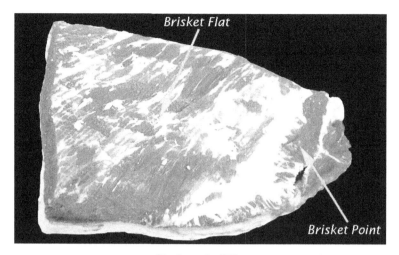

Brisket Flat

Brisket Point

Point & Flat

A packer brisket has two parts, the flat, and the point. The "flat" runs *the whole length of the brisket* (slice this against the grain and serve as brisket) while the "point" is a cap that sits on top of one end.

It's that cap, or "point" you want to use for your burnt ends.

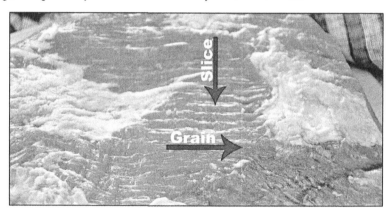

Slice

Grain

Slicing Brisket

The most perfectly smoked brisket will be tough and stringy if sliced wrong (with the grain.) The tricky park is that the grain of the point and flat run in different directions.

First, cut the front portion of the flat, pencil-thin and against the grain until you reach the point.

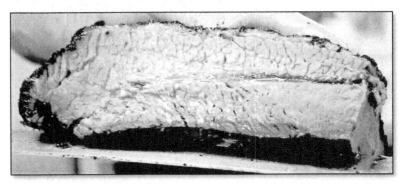

Then separate the point and the remaining piece of the flat along the thick seam of fat between the two muscles.

This allows you to slice each of the two muscles against the grain, and insures maximum tenderness from your brisket. .

Reheating Brisket

Spritz the meat with apple juice and add 1/8" of the same juice to the bottom of the pan. Cover tightly with foil and heat in a 200-250°F oven until warmed to your liking. Just before serving, brush on a thin layer of your favorite barbecue sauce to give the slices a nice sheen.

If you prefer to keep the cooked brisket whole and unsliced, wrap it in foil and refrigerate. Before reheating, open the foil and add some juice or broth as described above, and close the foil tightly. Heat in the oven or smoker at 200-250°F until warmed to your liking, then slice and serve.

Caja China Brisket

- *1 full packer brisket (10-12lbs), trimmed   16 oz Apple Juice or Cider*
- *½ cup Kosher salt, coarse   ½ cup black pepper, coarse grind*

Buy an untrimmed (*sometimes called packer style*) brisket available at most grocery stores. It will have a thick cap of fat, and is usually in heavy plastic packaging.

Three 14-pound briskets fit nicely in La Caja China; briskets are available in sizes from about 8 pounds and up. Calculate about 2 servings per pound.

Don't underestimate quantity, as you probably won't have much left over!

Preparing:

If you have a frozen brisket, let it thaw in the refrigerator for 2 days to defrost thoroughly.

The night before you plan to begin cooking, rinse the briskets, and pat dry.

Trim excess fat (*leave at least ¼ inch*).

Place the briskets in large disposable pans and generously apply salt, pepper, and granulated garlic to all meat surfaces.

Refrigerate overnight.

One hour before cooking, remove the briskets from the fridge and let stand at room temperature until cooking time.

Place your briskets in 3 disposable drip pans in the bottom of the box, and place the over-sized grill on top of these.

Add a couple of cups of water, apple juice, or beer to each pan.

Remove the end rails for ventilation.

Prep your smoking method with oak, mesquite, or a combination.

Cover box with the ash pan and charcoal grid.

Add 16 lbs. of charcoal for a 70# box or 18lbs of charcoal a 100# box, in two equal piles and light.

After 20 minutes, spread the coals evenly over the surface of the charcoal pan.

Cooking time starts right now. Smoke 1 hour, then add 8 lbs. of charcoal

After 1 hour (1st hour) open the box, flip briskets over, connect the wired thermometer probe in the thickest part of the center brisket, close the box.

Lift the charcoal grid shake it well to remove the ashes, now place it on top of the caja's long handles, or on two metal sawhorses.

Do NOT place on the grass or asphalt!

Use a large metal scoop to remove, and dispose of, the ashes.

Replace the charcoal grid, and add 10 lbs. of charcoal Continue to add 10 lbs. of charcoal, and remove ashes, every hour.

IMPORTANT: DO NOT PEEK! Only lift the charcoal lid as instructed.

Crutch

When your briskets reach 160F, open the box and remove them.

Wrap each in a double layer of heavy foil and return to the box. Add 10lbs of charcoal. Let the briskets cook, wrapped like this, until the internal temp reaches 195F (*4-6 more hours.*)

Note: You can also do the crutch in a pre-heated (225F) oven.

Remove briskets from heat, still foiled, wrap each in a towel, and set them in a cooler and rest at least one more hour. After resting, remove foil and move the brisket to your cutting board. Slice, pencil-thin, across the grain.

Tip: Only slice as much brisket as you plan to serve at *that* meal.

Reheating:

- Spritz the meat with apple juice and add 1/8" of the same juice to the bottom of the pan.
- Cover tightly with foil and heat in a 200-250°F oven until warmed to your liking.
- Just before serving, brush on a thin layer of your favorite barbecue sauce to give the slices a nice sheen.

If you prefer to keep the cooked brisket whole and unsliced, wrap it in foil and refrigerate. Before reheating, open the foil and add some juice or broth as described above, and close the foil tightly.

Heat in the oven or smoker at 200-250°F until warmed to your liking, then slice and serve.

Brisket Yield: When you take into account the trimming of the brisket before and after cooking, plus the shrinkage that occurs *during* cooking, don't be surprised if you end up with a 50% yield of edible meat from a whole, untrimmed brisket.

That means 6 pounds of edible meat from a 12 pound brisket.

Depending on the brisket and the internal temp you cook it to, it may be as low as 40% or as high as 60%.

If you're cooking brisket for a party, figure 4-5 ounces of meat per sandwich or 6 ounces of sliced meat on a plate (*8 ounces for hearty eaters*).

According to the Oxford English Dictionary, the English derivative of barbacoa, barbecue, *was first used in a book published in 1661 called "Jamaica Viewed."*

Sweet Chili Brisket

- *1 full packer brisket, trimmed*   *1 bottle of Thai Sweet Chili Sauce*
- *1/2 cup Kosher salt, coarse*   *1/2 cup black pepper, coarse grind*
- *2 cups Jasmine rice, cooked and hot*

Sweet chili sauce might be my all-time favorite condiment, and brisket is definitely in my top favorite meats. So, a thought stuck me the other day, out of the blue, *Hey, those two would be awesome together!*

Mix 1 cup of Thai sweet chili sauce with 1 cup of room temp water. Let rest 15-20 minutes, stirring occasionally, then strain out the solids and save the liquid. Inject the brisket (still in plastic) an ounce at a time, all over the brisket. Heavily salt and then smear all sizes of the brisket with 2 cups of undiluted chili sauce.

Refrigerate overnight.

Pre-heat your grill to high heat. Allow brisket to come to room temp (*about an hour*), remove from plastic, pat dry, and rub with salt and pepper. Sear brisket over direct heat, on both sides, until just beginning to char. Move to box, and smoke 7 hours, with oak wood .

At 7 hours, remove the brisket from the box, wrap tightly in foil, place in a pan, and cook another 7 hours in the box, or in a 225F oven, until the internal temp reaches 180F. Remove from oven or box, de-fat the juices, and mix ½ cup of de-fatted broth with ½ cup of chili sauce, reserving the rest of the broth for future recipes.

Remove foiled brisket from oven (and pan) and wrap in heavy towels. Place on the counter, or (*better*) in a cooler, and allow to rest 1 hour. Remove towel and foil, and rest another 30 minutes. Slice brisket thinly across the grain.

Serve over Jasmine rice, brushing the brisket slices with reserved broth/chili sauce mixture.

Black Pepper Mustard Brisket

- 1 full packer brisket (10-12lbs), trimmed   3 cups yellow mustard
- 2 Tbs. fine sea salt   1/2 cup Kosher salt, coarse
- 1 cup black pepper, coarse grind

Mix 1 cup of mustard sauce with 1 cup of room temp water, and fine sea salt.

While the brisket is still in plastic *(if it came in plastic)* inject sauce, an ounce at a time, all over the brisket. Refrigerate overnight.

Pre-heat your grill to high heat. Allow brisket to come to room temp *(about an hour)*, remove from plastic, pat dry, and smear generously with ½ of the remaining mustard, on all sides. Sprinkle heavily with salt and pepper.

Sear brisket over direct heat, on both sides, until just beginning to char. Move to box, and smoke 7 hours, with oak smoke. At 7 hours, remove the brisket from the box, smear the top with remaining mustard. Wrap tightly in foil, place in a pan, and cook another 7 hours in the box, or in a 225F oven, until the internal temp reaches 190F.

Remove foiled brisket from oven (and pan) and wrap in heavy towels. Place on the counter, or *(better)* in a cooler, and allow to rest 2 hours.

Slice brisket thinly across the grain, and serve.

Chef Perry's Brisket Beans

This is a great "next day" recipe after serving smoked brisket. My BBQ pal Chris saves the burnt ends from his briskets specifically for this recipe. Make sure you save the broth from the brisket pans as well. Chill it overnight and skim off the excess fat before adding to this recipe.

- 2-lb smoked brisket, cubed
- 2 C chopped onion
- 1 C bbq sauce*
- 2 Tbs yellow mustard
- 16oz kidney beans, drained
- 1 tsp smoked paprika
- 28oz baked beans
- 2 C brisket broth

1 lb sliced bacon, diced
1 C brown sugar
¼ C hot sauce*
1 tsp chili powder
1 tsp black pepper
16oz butter beans, drained
16oz diced tomatoes, drained

Sauté onions & bacon, add brisket cubes to warm.

Add all remaining ingredients (except beans), simmer 30 minutes.

Add beans, mix gently, and transfer into a heavy baking dish.

Bake at 350 for 1 hour, uncovered.

Note: My preferred brands for this recipe are Sweet Baby Rays Brown Sugar BBQ, and Frank's Red Hot Sauce.

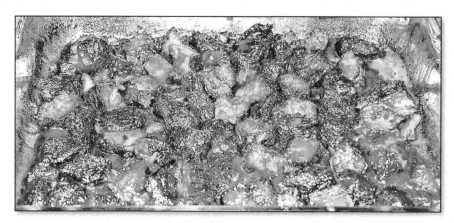

Kansas City Burnt Ends

Burnt ends are nearly always served on a bed of soft white bread, a side of pickle slices, and always with sauce. Coleslaw, potato salad, and baked beans are the favored sides.

- 4-5lbs smoked brisket point
- ½ C BBQ rub
- Hickory pellets or chips

Slice the point, against the grain, into 2in-thick "planks", and rub on all sides. Place the meat on a rack. Return the rack to the box and smoke for 1 hour, or until the meat is almost black on the outside. Brush with more sauce 15 minutes before it's done.

Transfer the meat to the carving board and let rest for 15 minutes.

Slice into cubes and serve, brushed with sauce, with bread & butter pickle slices and soft white bread.

Kansas City BBQ Sauce

Paul Kirk, BBQ guru, and a native of Kansas City, offers this recipe for his favorite burnt ends sauce:

- 3 cups ketchup
- ½ cup water
- ½ cup tomato paste
- 2 Tbsp chili powder
- 1 tsp salt
- 1 tsp garlic powder

2/3 cup dark brown sugar
½ cup white wine vinegar
2 Tbsp yellow mustard
1 Tbsp freshly ground pepper
1 tsp granulated onion powder
½ tsp ground ginger

In a medium saucepan, combine all of the ingredients and bring to a boil over moderate heat. Reduce the heat to low and simmer the sauce for 30 minutes, stirring often to prevent scorching.

The sauce can be refrigerated for up to 1 month.

Corned Beef Pastrami

I scored the "family secret" pastrami recipe from a VERY popular New York deli, just for *La Caja China Smoke!* I had to promise, on the soul of my children, not to reveal my source, but thank you Mikey, thank you Mikey's great-uncle, and thank you, LinkedIn! ;) This is a LONG process, but so completely worth it!

You'll need:

- 1 12-14lb lb beef plate*, navel, or brisket, trimmed of hard fat

Brine:

- 1/2 cup fine sea salt
- 4 Tbs. dark brown sugar
- 2 Tbs. curing salt
- 2-4 bay leaves
- 2 tsp. chopped garlic
- 1 tsp. coriander seeds

10 Tbs. granulated sugar
4 Tbs. honey
1 Tbs. ground mace
1 Tbs. ground ginger
2 tsp. mustard seeds

Spice rub

- 1 cup whole black peppercorns, coarsely ground
- 1 cup whole coriander seeds, coarsely ground

Hickory wood for smoking

In U.S. butchery, the belly, or "plate" of beef is a forequarter cut from the belly of the cow, between the brisket (in the front) and the flank. Like brisket, it's typically a cheap, tough, and fatty meat.

In a food-safe container large enough for the beef, combine sea salt, sugars, honey, curing salt, garlic, mace, ginger, mustard and coriander seeds with 12 cups warm water, whisking to dissolve the salt and sugar, add brisket, and more water to cover, if needed.

Weigh the meat down to make sure it stays completely submerged (*I use a large zip-bag filled with water to force the brisket to stay under*).

Refrigerate for 10-14 days, agitating the brine and turning the brisket every other day.

Note: *If you have access to a quality meat purveyor (NOT your chain grocery) that wet cures its own briskets for pastrami, you can skip the brining step, and go right to the overnight soak in water.)*

Remove brisket from brine, and soak in cold, clean water for 12 hours, or overnight, changing the water half-way through.

Seasoning

Remove the brisket from the water, pat it dry, and put it on a large baking sheet.

Coat evenly and generously on all sides with the ground peppercorns and coriander.

Refrigerate uncovered for at least 6 hours and up to 24 hours to air-dry the surface.

Smoking

Prepare the box to smoke at 200F (*starting with about a chimney and a half of coals, spread in the slightly to one side of the grate*).

Place the brisket fat side up on a rack over a foil-lined drip pan, slightly off-center on the other side of the box (*for more indirect heat*) and insert your temp probe, centered in the thickest part of the point. <u>I strongly recommend a second probe</u> to monitor box temp on this recipe, as letting the heat creep up will ruin a perfectly good pastrami.

Cover the box, and smoke (with hickory) 8-10 hours, or to an internal temp of 170F.

Remove the beef, wrap tightly in heavy foil, place in a pan and move to a pre-heated 200F oven. Cook until it registers 195°F on an instant-read thermometer inserted in the thickest part, 2 to 4 more hours.

Once the brisket reaches 195 degrees F. remove from heat and wrap tightly in foil and let it rest for a good 45 minutes. Refrigerate 24 hours.

To warm the whole brisket for serving, place it in a shallow hotel-pan, on a rack. Add beef stock and cover the pan with foil.

Place in a 250F. oven to steam. Whatever method you use, you will want to steam the brisket for about 2 hours on low heat.

To reheat by portion: steam slices in a vegetable steamer with beef stock, until warm, 2 to 3 minutes.

Serving

To serve, slice the pastrami pencil-thick against the grain (*if the meat is too tender, cut thicker*), halve these slices and pile ½ - ¾ lb. on a slice of dill-rye (*my favorite*) sandwich bread.

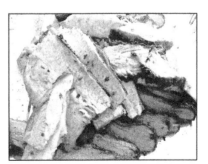

Smear the top slice with deli mustard, or horseradish, and serve with a big garlic pickle, and an ice-cold cream soda!

3 Rules for the Perfect Corned Beef Sandwich:

1. If you can fit your mouth around it, I made it wrong.

2. You can't leave until you finish it.

3. If you can finish it, I made it wrong.

~ The Carnagie Deli, NY

Beef Back Ribs in La Caja China

Yield: 6-8

Four five-bone racks beef back ribs

For the seasoning:

- 1 Tbsp beef base (*see notes*)   1 Tbsp garlic powder
- 1 Tbsp freshly ground black pepper   1 Tbsp smoked paprika
- 2 tsp sea salt   2 tsp light brown sugar
- 2 tsp chili powder

For the wrap:

- 1/2 cup honey   Warm water

Rub the beef base* into the ribs. Combine the remaining seasoning ingredients in a bowl, mixing well. Season the ribs on both sides and on the ends.

Wrap the ribs in plastic-wrap and refrigerate 24-36 hours.

Take the ribs out of the refrigerator 2 hours before you plan to start cooking. Un-wrap them and allow to rest at room temperature.

Start with 16 lbs. of charcoal (*about 3 Weber chimneys full*) for Model #1 Box or 18lbs. for Model #2 Box and light up the charcoal on top of the grid.

Once lit (20-25 minutes) spread the charcoal evenly over the charcoal grid. (Sear the ribs now.)

Prepare the top of La Caja China for indirect grilling. Allow both charcoal and any wood chunks to burn to white before adding the ribs. Put the meat on the well-oiled, preheated grill racks and cook, with the addition of wood chips of your choice, for 15-20 minutes per side, tent ribs loosely with foil while grilling.

Remove the ribs from the grill, and move to box in a single layer, bone side up on racks. Smoke at 250F.

After 1 hour (1st hour) add 9 lbs. of charcoal, and smoke for an additional 90 minutes.

Remove ribs from the box and wrap:

Put two large sheets of heavy-duty foil on top of each other and place one rack of ribs, top side up, on the foil.

Drizzle with 1 Tbsp. of honey and 1-2 Tbsp. of your favorite sauce (*see mine, below*) then sprinkle with up to 2 Tbsp. of cold water to moisten the rack.

Wrap ribs in foil to make a neat parcel, being careful not to pierce the foil with the bones. Repeat with the remaining ribs.

Return to ribs to the box (*meat side down*) and connect a wired thermometer probe in the thickest part of the meat, being careful it doesn't touch bone.

Put the foil parcels into La Caja China, rib side up, and cook (*do not add any more charcoal*) for one more hour, to an internal meat temp of 200F.

Remove the parcels, wrap (*foil and all*) in heavy towels, and allow to rest, for 30-45 minutes.

Unwrap the racks and discard the foil.

(*Optional: Put the ribs back on the grill and cook for 10 - 30 minutes to tighten the glaze and give the meat a bit more smoke.*)

Once the ribs have rested, place them on a cutting board, and slice between the bones in ¼ racks, or individual ribs.

Serve with warm sauce on the side.

Notes:

*Beef base is concentrated stock in liquid form, typically found in supermarkets and gourmet stores. It gives an added depth of flavor and richness. Optionally, you can boil down stock from beef bones yourself, or cheat and use packaged beef au jus. I have found Better Than Bullion to be the best brand out there.

**Beef Rib Sauce - Yes, I make my own "secret sauce" but, just as often, I use this and it's almost as good - Combine 2 cups of you favorite bottled sauce (Mine is Sweet Baby Rays Brown Sugar) with 1 cup apple juice and 1 cup cider vinegar. Add 1 Tbs dry rub, and a dash of hot-sauce (I like Frank's Red Hot.) Slowly simmer, stirring 40-60 minutes until thickened.

Traditional Mexican Barbacoa

This is a dish that I had twenty-five years ago, on a missions trip to Mexico.

I've spent the two and a half decades since, talking about those wonderful "beef tacos" we had at a tiny tortilleria in Trinidad Valley, where the corn tortillas were hot off a centuries-old stone tortilla oven, and bemoaning that I couldn't find anything like them here in the states.

Last night I followed this thousand-year-old recipe for barbacoa and, quite unexpectedly, realized, "That's it!"

The ancient dish of barbacoa, which is where we get the word "barbecue," runs deep within the culture of Mexico.

A popular Mexican way of eating barbacoa is having it served on a warm soft taco style corn tortilla with guacamole and salsa for added flavor; the meat or the tacos are often served in the banana leaves they were cooked in. It is also eaten with onions, diced cilantro and a squirt of lime juice.

Throughout Mexico, from pre-Mexican times to the present, barbacoa *(the name derives from the Caribbean indigenous Taino barabicu – or Sacred Fire Pit)* was the original Mexican barbecue, utilizing the many and varied moles *(pronounced "MO'-less", from Nahuatl molli)* and salsa de molcajete, which were the first barbecue sauces.

Game, turkey, and fish along with beans and other side dishes were slow cooked together in a pit for many hours.

Following the introduction of cattle, pigs, goats, sheep, and chickens by the Spanish, the meat of these animals was cooked utilizing the traditional indigenous barbacoa style of cooking.

"Barbacoa" actually has its origins in all the countries that and other Indian populations inhabited, not just Mexico. The Tainos themselves were pre-Columbian Indians located throughout the Caribbean and which some believe included the Arawak Indians who especially dominated the most lea-ward Caribbean islands themselves.

"The Arawak were first and foremost those who historically used the green and fire-resistant flexible branches of the giant Bearded Fig Tree (Los Barbadoes) to cook meats and fish over an open fire while first marinating their foods in tropical herbs and spices found naturally throughout the southern islands to South America." (Wikipedia)

In the original, Indian pit-cooking process, the meat was seasoned, and wrapped in either maguey or banana leaves.

Next, it was placed on a grill over a cauldron of water that is set over glowing coals in a pit about three feet deep.

The following recipe uses beef for the barbacoa, and takes a bit less time to cook.

You can use a bone-in pork shoulder, too.

Oh, and no need to dig a hole with this recipe!

BTW, if you can find a Hispanic market that makes fresh corn and flour tortillas (*we have one here in town*), find it. You'll never go back to those tasteless, pasty imitations at the grocery store!

Or, even better, make your own!

Mexican Barbacoa

• 5 lbs. beef roast	1 qt cold water
• 5 – Chiles Ancho	5 cloves garlic
• 1 lg. onion, quartered	2 banana leaves
• 2 tamarind pods	2 lg. bay leaves
• 1 tsp cumin	3 Tbs fresh cilantro, chopped
• Easy guacamole	2 dozen fresh tortillas

Build a single-zone fire and grill beef for 10 minutes per side until starting to char.

Move the roast into the box and smoke, with mesquite, for 2 hours at 225F

Drape 2 banana leaves over a "deep-dish" disposable pan, pressing to the bottom, then add a layer of chopped onion.

Remove roast from the box and place in the pan on top of the onion, then add the cold water, chiles ancho, tamarind, cumin, bay leaves and garlic, fold banana leaves over the top and secure with a couple of toothpicks.

Place the pan inside the box and add 10lbs of coals. Wait one hour and then add 5lbs of coals every hour for 6 hours.

Remove barbacoa from the box and allow to rest at least 30 minutes, then fish out the bones, ancho chiles, bay leaves, and tamarind pods. Remove the banana leaves.

Pour off fluids, and place the pan, uncovered, back on the grill for about an hour to let the juices reduce and thicken.

Stir frequently.

Just before bringing to the table, stir in most of the chopped Cilantro.

Serve with Easy Guacamole (see "Sauces), your favorite salsa, and hot tortillas.

If you're a chile-head, roast some whole jalapeños over the coals, slice, core (to remove the seeds) and serve on the side.

Baltimore Pit Beef
Smoked on the Grill

In East Baltimore, they've specialized in their own little piece of smoky meat history since the early 1970s. They call it...*pit beef.*

Now, two things we need to be clear on, right up front, "BBQ" Pit Beef is neither BBQ, nor is it cooked in a pit. It's basically the best roast beef sandwich you've ever eaten, with a lovely fire and smoke aroma that brings people from all over the country to Maryland.

To make this now-classic sandwich, Chefs use an eye of round, or bottom round roast flat cut from the hind quarter of the beef. Just to be difficult, I used a 7-blade chuck roast, because...well, I had one.

So, it's grilling with smoke, *not* BBQ. But, far more importantly…it's *unbelievably delicious!*

Here's how I make it:

- 2 tsp. fine sea salt   1 tsp. coarse black pepper
- 1 tsp. garlic powder   ½ tsp. chili powder
- One 3-pound cut of beef   8 potato rolls/16 slices of white bread
- ½ cup horseradish sauce   1 large sweet onion, thin rings & halves

Trim excess fat and any silver skin from the roast.

Mix salt, black pepper, garlic powder and chili powder in a small bowl.

Rub the beef all over with all the spice mixture (*don't forget the sides*), wrap with plastic wrap, and refrigerate overnight.

An hour before you're ready to start cooking, unwrap the roast, and let it rest on the counter, to bring the beef to room temp.

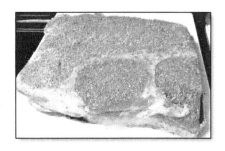

While the roast is resting, fire up a chimney full of coals. Once those are evenly grey, prepare a single-zone fire, slightly larger than the size of your roast, on your La Caja China for direct grilling.

NOTE: *To test the heat of your fire, you should be able to hold your hand about 5 inches above the coals for no more than 3 or 4 seconds.*

Oil your top grill(s) and set them over the coals and let them heat 1-2 minutes.

Set the roast over direct-heat, and grill (*uncovered*) for 2 to 3 minutes, flip and repeat until the exterior becomes evenly crusty.

Now, divide your coals, leaving a gap a little larger than the roast, in the middle.

Move the beef to this indirect-heat space, and cover with a roasting pan lid, or disposable pan (*as pictured*).

I like to toss a small handful of oak chips or pellets on the coals, every 10 minutes, just to get a little more smoky flavor.

I'm a big fan of oak for almost any beef dish, but cherry, hickory, or mesquite work well, too.

Grill for around a half-hour (*for medium-rare, after resting*), covered, or until a probe thermometer in the center reaches 130F.

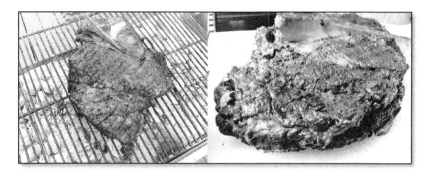

Move the beef to a cutting board; rest the meat for 5 minutes, then slice it against the grain <u>as thinly as possible, or shred.</u> Don't worry about full. pretty slices...it's all getting piled on the bun.

Pile the meat onto buns or bread. Top with horseradish sauce, and a few white onion slices.

BTW, this makes an amazing quick lunch for the pit-masters, while a piggy's roasting inside the box!

Magic Box Prime Rib

The traditional preparation for a standing rib roast is to rub the outside of the roast with salt and seasonings and slow-roast with dry heat. In the United States, it is common for barbecue purists to apply smoke to the uncooked rib roast at low heat for 2-3 hours before dry roasting.

In the United Kingdom, Yorkshire pudding is frequently served as a side dish with prime rib

- ½ C coarsely ground black pepper
- 2/3 C kosher salt
- 2 head of garlic, peeled
- ¼ C fresh rosemary
- 2 Tbsp. smoked paprika powder
- ½ C olive oil
- 1 – 5-6-pound prime rib roast (*6 bones*).

In a food processor, combine the salt, pepper, garlic cloves, rosemary and paprika, and process until fine. Add the olive oil and pulse to form a paste. Pat the rib roast dry with a paper towel or napkin.

Place the prime rib roast on a cutting board, bone-side up and rub with 1 Tbsp. of the salt paste.

Pack the salt paste all over the fatty surface of the roast, pressing to help it adhere. Let the prime rib stand at room temperature for 2 hours.

Insert meat thermometer so tip is in thickest part of beef, not resting in fat or touching bone.

Place disposable pans beneath the Caja China rack to catch the drippings, tent ribs loosely with foil, fire up your smoke box (*I use oak*), and close the roasting box.

Add 16 lbs. of charcoal for model #1 or 20 lbs. for model #2 or Semi-Pro Box, divided into two piles, and light up. At 30 minutes, spread coals over surface. Cooking time starts now.

At 1 hour (cooking time), lift the lid and quickly baste the roasts, and re-tent with foil. Dump excess ashes, close La Caja China and add another 10lbs of unlit coals. After 2 hours (*cooking time*), – baste again, remove the foil, and close the box to brown the top of the roasts.

Cook until rib roasts reach an internal temperature of 120 degrees F. Then remove the foil and brown 10 to 15 minutes longer. Remove the roasts from La Caja China, cover with aluminum foil, transfer the roasts to a large carving board, and let the meat rest for 30 minutes

Remember, the rib roast will continue to cook as it sets. The temperature will rise from 125 degrees F to 130-135 degree internal temperature (medium rare) at 15 in 20 minutes.

If allowed to rest as long as an hour, the temperature will rise even higher.

Carefully lift the salt crust off the meat and transfer to a bowl. Brush away any excess salt.

To remove the roast in one piece while keeping the rib rack intact, run a long sharp carving knife along the bones, using them as your guide.

Carve the prime rib roast 1-inch thick and serve, passing some of the crumbled salt crust as a condiment.

Cabrito Al Pastor
(whole roasted goat)

Cabrito is a word of Spanish origin, referring specifically to young, milk-fed goat. Despite being classified as red meat, goat is leaner and contains less cholesterol and fat than both lamb and beef; therefore it requires low-heat, slow cooking to preserve tenderness and moisture.

- 1 goat 40-45lbs
- 1 C rice vinegar
- 3 Tbs White onions, chopped
- 3 Tbs Cilantro, finely chopped
- Frijoles de Olla (*see recipe*)
- 16 Totopos (*crisply fried -tortilla wedges*)

½ C Sea Salt
2 C Guacamole
1 C Tomato, fine chopped
3 Tbs Serranos, fine chopped
1½ C Monterey Jack, grated

Brine cabrito in water, half of the salt, and vinegar for 2 hours. Rub the interior with remaining salt, onions, cilantro, and serrano peppers. Place the cabrito between the racks, tie using the 4 S-Hooks, and place inside the box, ribs side up.

Connect the wired thermometer probe in the thickest part of the leg, be careful not to touch the bone. Start smoker with apple.

Cover box with the ash pan and charcoal grid. Add 16 lbs. of charcoal for Model #1 Box or 18lbs. for Model #2 or Semi Pro Box and light up. Once lit (20-25 minutes) spread the charcoal evenly over the charcoal grid.

Cooking time starts right now.

After 1 hour (*1st hour*) open the box flip the cabrito over (ribs down) close the box and add 9 lbs. of charcoal.

After 1 hour (*2nd hour*) add 9 lbs. of charcoal. Do not add any more charcoal; continue cooking the meat until you reach the desired temperature reading on the thermometer.

IMPORTANT: Do not open the box until you reach the desired temperature.

To serve, cut cabrito in pieces, and place on plates. Garnish with guacamole, and more fresh onion, tomato, cilantro, and chiles.

Carving a whole lamb can be intimidating, so take it in sections. You'll need a large area to work with and several serving dishes or big pans.

Cut away the hind legs, then the forelegs. From here you can start carving up the individual sections.

The meat will be very tender, so slicing should not be a problem.

Fresh Lamb: Rare 140, Medium Rare 145, Medium 160

Serve with refried beans sprinkled with cheese, Totopos, and Pico de Gallo sauce.

Makes 8 servings.

My favorite way to eat smoked lamb or goat! I simple street-taco of meat, chopped white onion, cilantro, and a little hot sauce. Nothing better!

Moroccan Whole Roast Lamb
Recipe by Dee Elhabbassi

Cooking a whole lamb is as much an event, as it is a meal.

With a little planning and preparation, it's no more complicated than cooking a whole pig. Plan on about 4 pounds of raw weight for each guest.

1 – Grass-fed, three-month-old lamb around 36-40 pounds, skinned. Remove as much surface fat removed as possible.

• 4 sweet onions, pureed	2 C fresh garlic, ground
• 2 C butter	2 C olive oil
• Salt to taste	3 bunches cilantro, diced
• ¼ C cumin	½ C coriander seed
• ½ C paprika	2 Tbs fresh black pepper

Combine all chermoula ingredients and mix together over medium heat until it forms a paste. (*Chermoula is a ubiquitous Moroccan marinade.*)

Allow chermoula to set overnight.

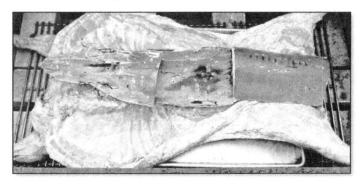

Rub this mixture over the surface of the lamb making sure to get it evenly distributed, inside and out. Plan on allowing the chermoula to sit on the meat for 48 hours before you cook.

Place the lamb between the racks, tie using the 4 S-Hooks, and place inside the box, ribs side up. Insert a wired thermometer probe into the thickest part of the leg, being careful not to touch the bone.

Note: *I like to run a couple of layers of soaked banana leaves up the spine of my lambs, to keep the tenderloins from overcooking or burning.*

Cover box with the ash pan and charcoal grid.

Add 16 lbs. of charcoal for Model #1 Box or 18lbs. for Model #2 Box and light up.

Once lit (*20-25 minutes*) spread the charcoal evenly over the charcoal grid. Cooking time starts right now.

After 1 hour (*1st hour*) open the box flip the lamb over (*ribs down*) close the box and add 9 lbs. of charcoal.

After 1 hour (*2nd hour*) add 9 lbs. of charcoal.

Do not add any more charcoal; continue cooking the meat until you reach the desired temperature reading on the thermometer. I cook mine to 140F (*rare*).

IMPORTANT: Do not open the box until you reach the desired temperature.

Carving a whole lamb can be intimidating, so take it in sections. You'll need a large area to work with and several serving dishes or big pans.

Cut away the hind legs, then the forelegs. From here you can start carving up the individual sections.

The meat will be very tender, so slicing should not be a problem.

Fresh Lamb: Rare 140, Medium Rare 145, Medium 160

Easter Smoked Leg of Lamb

In Greece, Easter is the biggest holiday of the year, and apparently most everyone roasts a whole lamb on a "Souvla" which is a large spit. This is a popular recipe around the north of Madrid, as well, especially during the holiday seasons. Sweet, succulent leg of lamb is one of the world's great culinary treats.

- 2 - 9 lb legs of lamb (*bone in*)   Freshly ground black pepper
- 2 tsp. fresh thyme   2 C of dry white wine
- 2 Tbsp of wine vinegar   Springs of fresh rosemary
- 4 Tbsp of olive oil   Salt
- 4 cloves of garlic sliced   4 C of water
- Juice of 1 lemon

Set the legs on a roasting rack, in a roasting pan, and rub with half of the olive oil. Season the legs with salt and pepper and rub the thyme over the surface.

Let the lamb sit for an hour, at room temperature, to absorb the flavors.

Put the white wine, water, vinegar and lemon juice into a pan and bring to the boil. Allow to cool.

Make some slits in the leg of lamb and put some slices of garlic, and springs of rosemary into them, baste with ½ of the liquid, and then rub the lamb with the rest of the olive oil.

Fill a smoker box, or tube, with hickory pellets, and light. Be sure to remove the two end rails from your roasting box, to allow for proper ventilation.

Light your charcoal and allow the box to heat up. Then set the lamb legs, rack, and pan in the bottom, add your smoker, and close the roasting box.

Roast the legs of lamb for approximately 3 hours, add fresh charcoal every hour as per the instructions on the side of your roaster. After 3 hours, check the meat, cover any hotspots with foil, and add fresh charcoal in order to increase the temperature of the box.

Roast the legs of lamb for another 20 minutes until brown, then check the internal temperature of the meat.

Med Rare: 145
Med: 160

After the meat is cooked, toss it on the top grill, over the coals, to crisp the outsides, let rest 20 minutes, tented in foil, then slice and serve it with the side dishes of your choice.

If you take the lamb off at 140°F and let it rest for 20 minutes tented with foil the interior of the lamb should reach 145°F, which is medium rare.

Kalo Pashcha! (*Happy Easter!*)

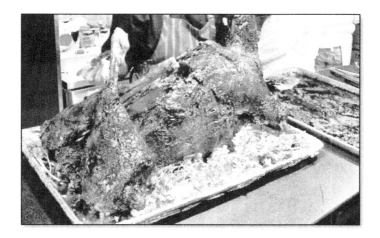

Greek Smoke Roasted Goat

For much of the world, goat is *the* red meat, and I LOVE roasting goat in my La Caja China!

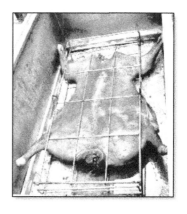

I'd suggest a box temp of 250F for about four hours, until almost done (160F). Then place goat over the coals of a low mesquite fire, on the LCC grilling rack, to sear and crisp. Baste with the butter sauce and let it smoke until tender and done (170-175F), maybe another 20 minutes.

As far as internal temp of your goat: "Cook all raw goat beef steaks, chops, and roasts to a minimum internal temperature of 145 °F as measured with a food thermometer before removing meat from the heat source." – *So sayeth the USDA.*

Of course, they then say, in the very next line, "allow meat to rest for at least three minutes before carving or consuming" – which simply proved that they don't know their…goat…from a hole in the ground.

If you pull a whole roast goat (*or any other animal*) off the heat, and don't leave it the heck alone for at LEAST 20 minutes, tenting loosely in foil, you should be sentenced to live on McRib sandwiches and gas-station corndogs the rest of your life.

Oh, and for goats I like a simple wet rub of salt, olive oil, and fresh rosemary.

PORK

Pork (*meat from a domestic pig*) is the most eaten animal protein in the world. Humans have been raising pigs for food since 5000 BC, eating it both fresh and preserved in various ways, most often by curing. Pork is especially prized in Asian cooking for its fattiness and luxurious texture.

Over the last half-century, pigs have been bred to be much leaner, with more protein and lower in calories, saturated fat, and cholesterol than the pork produced previously.

Here are the basic cuts of pork, and some favorite ways to prepare them:

Ham

The ham is the upper portion of a pig's hind leg. Hams can be found fresh, but most are cured with brine, and smoked, which imparts a meatier, more intense flavor.

Bone-in ham, like most meats typically has more flavor than boneless.

Ham can be slow-smoked, brushed with a sweet/spicy sauce, and finished in the oven to set the glaze.

Loin

A large cut (*from the back*), pork loi n has no bones, making it easy to slice.

With a dense texture and tons of flavor from a large fat cap, pork loin is ideal stuffed, as in this porchetta, and roasted.

It's also a very economical cut to portion into chops for grilling and smoking.

Pork Loin Porchetta, big bold Italian flavors make this my personal favorite!

Pork Chops

The best chops are cut from the center of the loin. The first are loin chops; looking like miniature T-bone steaks, they still have a bit of tenderloin on them, and have tons of flavor.

Second are the rib chops, cut without the tenderloin. These are a moody cut and can overcook and dry out if not closely watched. Chops cut thinner than an inch thick are extremely difficult to grill properly.

Tenderloin

Tenderloin is one of the most popular cuts of pork in the United States, likely because they are quick and easy to prepare.

Quite lean and tender, this cut is long, narrow, and tapers at one end.

Tenderloin is quite a bit smaller that the pork loin, and a great choice for a quick dinner, after a day-long marinade.

Baby Back Ribs

These curved, meaty slabs come from high on the ribcage near the backbone. Sweet and juicy meat, this is a favorite cut.

Back-backs grill quickly. For best results, go with no more than a 2-pound rack.

Spare Ribs

From the underbelly of the pig, and with a bit less meat than baby-backs, spare ribs are still quite tasty, with a lot of fat to keep them moist and juicy.

A full rack of spare ribs weights 3-4 pounds.

I typically rub ribs with spices, and smoke in the caja for an hour or so. Then, I wrap them in foil and roast them for another couple of hours, before finishing them (*unfoiled*) over the coals.

Pork Belly

Hugely popular in the culinary world right now, pork belly, starts out from the underside (*belly*) of the pig.

Belly doesn't mean "stomach", but the layer of meat and fat on the underside of the pig.

Pork belly is the cut that we get bacon from, once it's cured, smoked and sliced.

Pork Belly Porchetta

With a crispy skin and unctuous umami layers of meat and fat, less is more with pork belly, which makes it great as an appetizer, or a garnish for soups or salads. If you'd rather go "over the top", the spiced and rolled Pork Belly Porchetta (*above*) is my favorite way to use this divine cut of pork.

Pork Hock

A pork hock (ham hock) is a cut from the pig's leg just below the knee. Pork hock is a very inexpensive and tough piece of meat that is loaded with connective tissue, ligaments and muscle fibers.

Once throw away food, it was (as many of our best dishes) adopted by slaves and servants who discover that, when cooked low and slow, it produces a tender meat and a delicious stock that's a perfect base for stews and soups.

Pork hocks are typically available either smoked or unsmoked. I prefer them smoked, as my favorite use for them is to slowly simmer them in a pot of beans and onions, until the meat falls off the bone. Serve this with hot cornbread, and you'll have a meal that far surpasses its humble origins.

Boston Butt (Shoulder)

Boston butt (*pork butt*) is what we Americans call the cut of pork that comes from the upper part of the shoulder, on the front leg of the pig.

Typically, it's sold bone-in.

This is most common cut for pulled pork BBQ.

Slowly smoked at low heat (225F) for 12-14 hours, the tough collagen in the shoulder becomes gelatin, producing a juicy, and extremely tender pulled pork.

Picnic Shoulder

Another prime choice for pulled pork, the less fatty picnic shoulder cut is a tougher piece of meat than the Boston butt, requiring the same "low and slow" cooking approach.

Often sold boneless, the picnic provides more meat than the Boston, but can also be less flavorful (when you have the option, always cook meat bone-in for additional flavor!)

Pork Cheek

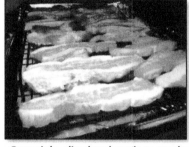

Last, but certainly not least...my very favorite cut of pork. Pork cheeks are exactly what they sound like: a fist-sized piece of meat resting in the hollow of the pig's cheekbone.

Guanciale, which I cook with often, is a bacon made from the cheeks and the jowls.

Guanciale, sliced and ready to smoke

Lean, yet moist, and loaded with collagen, a low roast or simmer will produce a baseball size piece of heavenly meat that is fork-tender and bursting with savory pork goodness.

Besides one-upping bacon in your favorite recipes, pork cheek, slowly braised in red-wine and tomato sauce makes and amazing start to the best marinara sauce you've ever tasted!

Peach-Ginger Smoked Holiday Ham

I love just about any combination of spicy and sweet, and this peach-ginger glazed ham recipe is no exception.

My wife has informed me that this is the *only* ham recipe I am to use for Easter, from now on! ☺

- 1 (10 pound) fully-cooked, bone-in ham
- 2 Tbs Dijon mustard
- 3/4 cup packed brown sugar
- 2 tsp. fresh ginger root. Minced

2 cups peach preserves

2 Tbs soy sauce

1/4 cup apple cider vinegar

1/2 cup apple juice

Unwrap the ham and place it, cut-side down, on a flat roasting rack.

Start you La Caja China with 15lb of charcoal, and pre-heat the interior to 300F (*lid closed*). Place the ham (*on the roasting rack*) in the bottom of the roaster, over a pan of hot water, replace lid, and smoke with hickory for 1 hour.

While the ham is smoking, mix together the mustard, brown sugar, cider vinegar, soy sauce, apple juice and peach preserves in a saucepan over medium heat. Bring to a low boil and then stir in the ginger.

Reduce heat, and simmer until the sauce has thickened, 25 to 30 minutes. Set aside and keep warm.

Place the ham, rack and all, on a foil lined baking sheet, using enough foil to wrap the entire ham.

Baste ham heavily with 1/3 the peach glaze. Wrap in foil, and return to box. Continue roasting to an internal temperature of 140 degrees, 1-1/2 hours more.

30-45 minutes before the ham is done, uncover it, baste again with another 1/3, and continue roasting to "set" the glaze. You can add more hickory smoke at this point, of you like.

Remove ham from La Caja China and bring it (*on the rack & pan*) inside. Carefully turn the ham on its side, allowing the slice and fan. Brush liberally with the remaining glaze.

Tent loosely in foil, and let the ham rest for 15 minutes before carving.

Garlic Rosemary Pork Loin

I like to serve this with homemade apple sauce and garlic-mashed potatoes.

- ¼ C plus 2 Tbs. extra-virgin olive oil
- 20 garlic cloves, chopped
- 6 stems of rosemary, chopped
- ½ cup sea salt
- 2 Tbs. black pepper
- 8-10lb whole pork loin

In a small bowl combine ¼ cup olive oil, chopped garlic, rosemary, salt, and pepper. Rub all over the pork, including the top, bottom, and sides. Put the pork in a plastic bag. Marinate overnight in the fridge.

Take the loin out of the fridge and let stand at room temperature for 30 minutes. Brush off as much marinade as you can.

Sear the outsides of pork loin briefly directly over the coals (*about 10 minutes, total.*)

Transfer to a rack (*over a pan*) in the bottom of the box, load 14lbs charcoal, and hot smoke for 40 to 45 minutes, or until a thermometer registers 140°.

Transfer to a board and let rest for 15 minutes before slicing.

Slice thin and serve hot.

Cuban Mojo Pork Loin

- 1 Fresh Pork Loin, 8-10 lbs.
- 4 C Sour Orange Juice (or, 1 C lime juice and 3 C orange juice)
- 12 Lg. garlic cloves
- 2 Tbs. dried oregano leaves
- 2 tsp. ground black pepper
- 2 Tbs. salt
- 4 bay leaves

With a sharp knife, puncture pork in several places. Place in a shallow roasting pan.

In a food processor, puree ¼ cup of sour orange juice, garlic cloves, oregano, black pepper and salt; puree long enough to form a paste.

Rub paste all over pork, pushing mixture into punctured holes.

Add bay leaves to the rest of the sour orange juice and pour over pork.

Refrigerate and marinate for 6 hours.

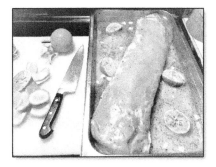

Take the loin out of the fridge and let stand at room temperature for 30 minutes.

Transfer to a rack (*over a pan*) in the bottom of the box, and hot smoke (350F) with mesquite for 2 hours, baste again, wrap loin in heavy foil, and return to box.

Roast another hour, or until a thermometer registers 145° (*it will be a little pink, and that's perfectly okay!*) ☺

Remove from box, unwrap, and rest 30 minutes before slicing.

Pork Loin Tacos with Cilantro Aioli

This is my favorite way to use leftover Mojo Pork Loin. In fact, sometimes I make *that*, just to make *this!*

- 2 C cooked pork loin, 1in cube
- 2 Tbs. chili powder
- 1 red bell pepper, diced
- 4 strips bacon, chopped
- 16oz fire-roasted diced tomatoes (*with juice*)

2 Tbs. cumin powder
1 C sweet corn kernels, fresh
1 white onion, diced
2oz diced green chilies
2 tsp. sea salt

Fry bacon in a skillet over medium-high heat (*do not drain*). Add onions and bell pepper and sauté until softened. Add corn, 1 Tbs. cumin, 1 Tbs. chili powder, and tomatoes. Cook until hot through, then transfer to slow-cooker.

Combine pork loin cubes with remaining seasonings, and stir to coat the meat. Add to slow cooker. Cook 4 hours on low. Spoon into tacos, and serve.

Tacos:

- 8 flour gorditas, warmed
- 8 Tbs Cilantro Aioli

8 Tbs fresh white onion, diced

Cilantro Aioli

- ½ C fresh cilantro, chopped
- 1 -3 drop hot pepper sauce
- ¾ C mayonnaise

½ lime, juiced
1 tsp. cumin

Combine all ingredients in a food processor, and mix until blended. Chill before serving.

Note: If you chop the pork even smaller (1/4 in. dice) this would make an amazing taco dip, with warm corn tortilla chips.

3-2-1 Ribs in La Caja China

Now don't get me wrong...I love my brisket and pulled pork, but a perfectly cooked slab of pork ribs, tender and juicy on the inside, with a sticky, crusty glaze, or a sweet/spicy dry rub...well, if God made anything better than that, He kept it for Himself.

I've cooked ribs many, many, many ways over the last 40 years, and for my money, the most consistent and crowd-pleasing results come from the "3-2-1 Method."

In short, this method breaks down to a six-hour cook time:

- 3 hours in smoke, uncovered.
- 2 hours wrapped, cooking low and slow
- 1 hour of "finishing" over higher heat to finish the bark, or set the glaze.

But, like all things in life, however "simple", there are tips and techniques that mean the difference between "good" ribs, and a dinner that is spoken of in hushed and reverent tones to future generations.

BEFORE adding seasonings or rub, use a spoon and a paper-towel to remove the membrane from the back of the ribs. This membrane is like nature's plastic wrap, blocking your rub from permeating the ribs from both sides.

Apply your seasonings or rub to both sides of the ribs, generously, the night before.

Basically you're dry-brining, drawing the internal moisture out of the meat, before reversing engines and pulling all that moisture back in, along with the flavor and tenderizing properties of the salt & sugar combo.

If you don't believe this, apply the rub and wait a few minutes as the puddles of liquid form in the hollows of the ribs (*have your plastic-wrap already underneath so it doesn't escape!*) wrap the racks tightly in a double layer, and place in the fridge, meat side down (this helps with the reabsorption process).

The next day, when you un-wrap your ribs, take note that there is little or none of that moisture left visible outside of the ribs.

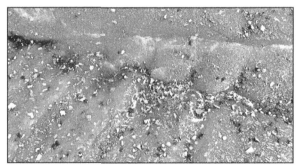

Seasoning ribs just shortly before cooking will pull out moisture, without allowing time for it to be reabsorbed. That's a bad thing.

Like any other meat, you want your ribs to be an even temperature, from the surface to the bone, before cooking. Thawed ribs, set on the kitchen counter, will take around 45 minutes to reach ready-to-cook temp.

Put some disposable pans in the bottom of the box, and add a few inches of hot water (*cold liquid is a heat-suck.*)

Some folks swear by the tenderizing properties of using beer instead of water, but I really haven't noticed much of difference. Everyone's taste buds are different though, so try it yourself!

By the way, you want this additional moisture in the box because it helps seal in the moisture that's already in the ribs, instead of drawing it out.

Top 2-3 water pans with the oversized grill rack. Place your prepped ribs on the rack, and then fire up your smoking method. Carefully add the Caja lid and coal grate, covered with pre-lit and spread coals.*

Smoke your ribs for three hours, adding coals every hour. I like to use a temperature probe, through a halved lemon, to track the internal temperature of the box. Keep it between 225-240F.

The reason I pre-light and spread the coals is that lighting them in piles creates hot-spots on the meat. THIS IS WHAT I DO, AND IT MAY NOT BE THE SAFEST METHOD (there, now hopefully I won't get a phone call from my lawyer.)

Alternatively, you can use a couple of charcoal chimneys to prep your coals, and then spread them as soon as you add them to the top. That's probably what the smart people do.

After the first three hours the ribs are, of course, completely cooked...but they would be pretty tough and chewy if you served them right now.

This is where the 3-2-1 method incorporates a pro-bbq method we talked about earlier, commonly called "The Texas Crutch." Remove the ribs from the box and wrap each rack separately (*and tightly*) in heavy foil, adding a good amount of mop, or (*what I like*) a 50/50 combo of heated apple juice and apple-cider vinegar, then closing them up and rolling the ends of the foil to get a good seal.

This method is controversial among professional pit-masters, but I like really tender (but not quite fall-off-the-bone) ribs, and this is how I get them. So, there's that.

Return your ribs to the box, re-cover, and cook another two hours.

Be sure to check out my full "3-2-1 Ribs" video at **homechefvideos.com**

Now, unwrap your ribs, and move them to the top grills, flesh side down, for another 45 minutes. DO NOT add more charcoal prior to this step. I don't even shake the ashes off first.

How do you know your ribs are done?

There are two fool-proof methods. First, on a well-cooked rack of ribs, the meat at the end of the bones will have pulled back at least 1/4 inch, exposing the bones. Once you see this, grab a toothpick, and poke it between two of the center ribs.

There should be just a little bit of resistance when the ribs are done.

Now we come to decision time...you can finish them as "dry ribs" (*which is a terrible term to use with ribs*) but means searing the meat on both sides, and adding additional dry rub just before serving.

Alternatively, you can sauce and glaze your racks with your favorite sauce, flipping often to "set" the glaze, without burning it.

If the temps of your coals has dropped a lot by this time, shake off the ashes and/or add just one more chimney of coals.

A touch of char is good, but a sweet sauce can make for a nasty charcoal crust on those beautiful ribs you just worked so hard on, so put down your phone and pay attention! 😉

Add your sauce in several thin layers, allowing each to set before reapplying.

Dry or wet, when the surface of the ribs is set, remove from the heat and allow to rest, tented loosely in foil for at least 15 minutes before cutting a serving.

Like anything else in life, from writing to building houses, perfection lay in two elements:

Practice, and Passion.

There's an old saying (*one I certainly can't take credit for*) that says:

"Cooking great BBQ comes from experience, and experience...that comes from cooking bad BBQ."

BBQ and grill as often as you can, don't be afraid to experiment (it's just one dinner, after all), and hyper-focus on the details...

- Did you search through the bin to find the very best-looking rack of ribs, from the best supplier in town?
- Is the rub balance between salty/sweet/spicy perfect?
- It the cooking temp exactly where you want it?

If that sounds a little OCD...it is.

Obsessive people win gold medals.

Carolina Gold Baby Back Ribs

Now, mustard barbecue sauces are completely different than your regular red sauces, obviously, but not just due to the mustard. They're also much, much tangier, especially the Carolina ones, than the average-joe sauces, too.

- 1 rack pork ribs, (*rinse, pat dry, remove sinew*)
- 1/2 Cup Dry Rub
- Mustard BBQ Sauce (*see below*)

Prep and rub your ribs, wrap in plastic wrap and place in the fridge overnight.

Place the ribs on the counter, unwrapped, an hour before you plan to start smoking.

Light your coals and let them burn until evenly grey, then move the lid off the box.

Top 2-3 water pans with the oversized grill rack. Place your ribs on the rack, and then fire up your smoking method. Carefully add the Caja lid and coal grate, and spread the coals.

Smoke your ribs for three hours, adding coals every hour.

I like to use a temperature probe, through a halved lemon, to track the internal temperature of the box. Keep it between 225-240F.

After three hours, remove the ribs from the box.

Place a large sheet of foil, several inches longer than the ribs at each end, onto working surface dull side-up. ribs, meat side-up, onto foil.

Coat generously with a little over half of the mustard sauce, on both sides.

Bring long-edged sides of foil up to meet and carefully roll down to meet the top of the ribs.

Fold ends of foil inward like an envelope and roll up. It should be a nice closed package touching the meat. Just be careful not to tear the foil. You want it sealed closed.

Place rib package onto foil-lined baking sheet folded side-up (meat side-down). Smoke for another 2 hours.

Remove ribs from foil, coat well with remaining sauce, and return the ribs, uncovered, and smoke for one last hour.

Remove ribs and rest, tented loosely in for, for 20 minutes before slicing and serving.

South Carolina Gold Sauce

- ½ Gal. yellow mustard
- 1 Cup light brown sugar
- ¼ Cup Worcestershire sauce
- ¼ Cup Louisiana hot sauce (*to taste*)

½ Gal. cider vinegar
2 Tbsp. sea salt
2 Tbsp. black pepper

For each of these sauce recipes, combine ingredients, heat to a low simmer, and cook 20-30 minutes, stirring often.

Chill for at least 24 hours *(72 is better)* before using.

Memphis Dry Ribs

Some of the most popular items on the Memphis menu, are actually referred to as "dry ribs" *(referring to lack of sauce, NOT thankfully, the quality of the Q!)* which *are* coated in a blend of spices, usually a combination of garlic, paprika, onions, cumin, with a few "secret" ingredients, that the cook would likely face down a firing squad before sharing with you.

These dry ribs *(usually Baby Backs)* are slowly smoked until falling off the bone and might *(might)* be served with some sauce on the side.

- 1 rack of baby-back ribs
- 1 tsp. ground cumin
- 1 tsp. chili powder
- 1 tsp. sugar
- 1 tsp. fresh black pepper

1/4 tsp. cayenne pepper
2 tsp. smoked paprika
1 tsp. dry oregano
1 tsp. salt
3 Tbs. vegetable oil

Mix the rub ingredients together well in a small bowl.

Remove the membrane from the bone side of the ribs. Place them in a large rimmed pan, and rub them on both sides with vegetable oil.

Pour 3/4 of the rub over the ribs and work the rub fully and evenly into the ribs.

Place your prepped ribs on a rack in the bottom of the box, and then fire up your smoking method, using hickory wood. Carefully add the Caja lid and coal grate, covered with pre-lit and spread coals.

Smoke your ribs for three hours, adding coals every hour, at a box temp between 225-240F. Wrap the ribs in foil and smoke another 2 hours. Unwrap and let rest 15 minutes before cutting.

Sprinkle with more rub, just before serving.

Texas Salt & Pepper Pork Belly

Salt, pepper and a long slow smoke creates an amazing belly with an intensely flavorful crust.

- 1/4 cup coarsely ground black pepper
- 3 tablespoons Kosher salt
- 1 4-5lb piece boneless pork belly, skin removed
- Medium smoking wood, such as oak or hickory

In a small bowl combine pepper and salt. Season pork belly all over liberally with this simple rub.

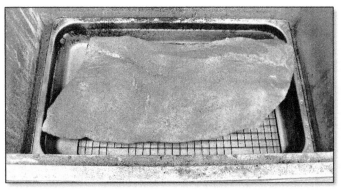

Preheat box to 225F, smoking with oak or hickory.

Place the pork belly in the box (*on a rack*) and smoke to 195-203F on an instant read thermometer, inserted into the thickest section of meat (6 to 8 hours), adding coals and removing ashes every hour to maintain a box temp of 225F.

Wrap the belly tightly in butcher paper or foil, place in a cooler or oven, and let rest for 2 hours.

Slice pork belly and serve.

Pork Belly Burnt Ends

Imagine if you married the perfectly smoked fatty-end of a Texas Brisket, to a succulent hunk of slow-roasted pork shoulder.

These would be their babies…

- 8lb Pork Belly skin removed   ½ C Pork Shoulder Rub
- 1 ½ sticks Butter, sliced   ½ C Brown Sugar
- ¼ cup Honey

Glaze:

- 1 C Sweet BBQ Sauce   ¼ cup Apple Juice
- ¼ cup Apple Jelly   1 Tbsp Frank's Hot Sauce

Combine all of the glaze ingredients in a small pan and simmer over medium heat until smooth. Allow to cool.

Preheat caja to 250F, using Cherry Wood for smoke. Rinse and dry pork belly, and cube into 1 ½" pieces. Season on all sides rub, arrange onto a rack (*not touching*), and place on grate in box.

Smoke belly for 2 – 2 ½ hours, adding coals every hour. Place cubes into a hotel pan and cover with brown sugar and honey.

Arrange butter in between the pork belly pieces. Cover pan with aluminum foil and return to smoker for 1 ½ hours or until the pieces are tender. Drain the liquid from the pan and add the glaze to the burnt ends.

Toss gently to coat each piece and return to the box to set the glaze for 5-10 minutes. Serve.

Pork Shoulders in La Caja China

Position the roasting box is a safe, well ventilated area (*but out of direct drafts*). If roasting on the lawn, be sure to water the grass well before cooking, just in case.

Place 3-4 (*depending on size*) disposable drip pans in the bottom of the box, and either place the over-sized grill on top of these, or pack each shoulder in a pan, on a rack.

Add a couple of cups of water, apple juice, or beer to each pan. Remove one of the top end rails for ventilation. Put prepped shoulders on the racks, fat side down. Insert the probe from a wired thermometer into one of the middle shoulders, and run wire under the rail of the top frame.

Place one of the top grills, or one pig rack over the center of the shoulders, light your smoker unit (pictured with the A-Maze-N Smoker) and place it on top of the top grill, over a small piece of foil to protect the bottom from moisture.

Cover box with the ash pan and charcoal grid. Add 16 lbs. of charcoal for a 70# box or 18lbs of charcoal a 100# box, in two equal piles and light. Once lit (*20-25 minutes*) spread the charcoal evenly over the charcoal grid.

Roast 1 hour, then add 8 lbs. of charcoal.

Add an additional 8 pounds of charcoal every hour until you reach 180 F on the meat thermometer.

IMPORTANT: DO NOT PEEK! Only lift the charcoal lid as instructed below.

Lift the charcoal grid shake it well to remove the ashes, now place it on top of the caja's long handles, or on two metal sawhorses.

Once you reach **195F**, repeat the steps to remove the ashes.

Open the box and remove the top grill and smoker. Flip the shoulders, fat-cap up, salt and score the skin using a very sharp knife, this helps to remove the fat and crisp the skin.

Cover the box again with the ash pan and the charcoal grid; do not add more charcoal at this time.

After 30 minutes, take a peek by lifting the charcoal pan by one end only. You will continue doing this every 10 minutes until the skin is crispy to your liking.

For sliceable pork, remove shoulders from Caja now and allow to rest 30 minutes.

For more of a Southern-style pulled pork, take the finished shoulders out of the box, wrap each tightly in 3 layers of foil, and roast in the oven (on a sheet pan), at **225F**, for an additional 4-6 hours.

Never use a smoker in an enclosed area or without proper ventilation.

Meat cooked in its own drippings will be mushy, so I always use a rack. It also helps the smoke to reach all sides of the meat.

Chef Perry's Pork Shoulder Rub
(per shoulder)

- ¼ C smoked paprika
- ¼ C light brown sugar
- 2 Tbs onion powder
- 2 Tbs coarse black pepper
- 1 tsp cayenne powder

¼ C coarse sea salt
2 Tbs garlic powder
2 Tbs Italian season
1 Tbs hickory salt

Apply the rub generously to the inside of a butterflied pork shoulders, roll it, and apply more rub to the outside.

You MUST allow the rubbed shoulders (or ribs) to rest in the fridge at least overnight so that the rub will help form that wonderful "bark" while roasting.

Finally, after it's done cooking and you've pulled, chopped, or shredded the meat with a little apple-cider vinegar, give it one last sprinkle for an intense, spicy flavor.

Serve on hotdogs buns (*less spillage than burger buns*), slider rolls, or go traditional and serve with soft sliced white bread.

Some folks will toss the shredded pork with a sauce, but I find that it overwhelms the flavor of the meat. I prefer to serve it with a thin, warmed sauce in a squirt bottle, on the side.

Peach Mojo Pork Shoulders

- 5-6lb pork shoulder (*I prefer the "Boston-butt" cut*)
- 1 quart Tropical Mojo (*see below*)
- ½ cup coarse sea-salt
- 2 Tbs garlic powder
- 1 Tbs red pepper flakes

Glaze:

- 12 oz peach preserves
- 15 oz canned sliced peaches in heavy syrup
- 2 Tbs. soy sauce
- 1 Tbs red pepper flakes

Toppings:

- 1 can pineapple rings, drained and patted dry
- 15 oz canned sliced peaches in heavy syrup, drained
- 4 oz macadamia nuts, crushed

Combine glaze ingredients in a large saucepan, and bring to a low simmer. Cook until reduced by 1/3, stirring often. Cool, and let sit in fridge overnight. Warm before using.

Inject the pork with mojo, and marinate overnight. Then, allow pork to come to room temp just before roasting.

Rub pork all over with sea-salt, garlic, and 1 Tbs of red pepper flakes.

Place shoulder(s) in La Caja China (fat down on racks) insert prober thermometer, and smoke with mesquite to an internal temp of 160F, at a box temp of around 225F, using 12lbs of charcoal.

Remove shoulders, place in a pan and coat heavily with 2/3 of the warm glaze. Wrap in heavy foil and return to box, in pan. Continue smoking to an internal temp of 195F.

Remove pan from box, and allow pork to cool/rest 15 minutes.

Chop (or pull) pork, discarding any bones, and return to pan.

Brush heavily with remaining glaze, top with pineapple rings and peach slices (*optional*), sprinkle with macadamia nuts and return to La Caja China.

Check every five minutes until browned to your liking.

Tropical Mojo

- ½ cup minced garlic (the wet stuff.)
- ¼ cup fine sea salt
- 1/8 cup black pepper, fine ground
- 2 Tbs dried Oregano
- 2 quarts orange juice
- 2 cups lime juice
- 1 quart pineapple juice

Mix all. Let sit at room temperature for 30 minutes or longer.

Cochinita Pibil

Cochinita pibil is a traditional Mexican slow-roasted pork dish from the Yucatán Peninsula.

Preparation involves marinating the meat in strongly acidic citrus juice, coloring it with annatto seed, and roasting the meat while it is wrapped in banana leaf.

Traditionally, cochinita pibil was buried in a pit with a fire at the bottom to roast it.

The Mayan word "pibil" means "buried."

- 3 – 8lb pork shoulders, cubed   ½ C fresh lime juice
- 3 – 4oz packages achiote seasoning   ¼ cup minced garlic
- 2 Tbs. dried oregano   2 Tbs. cumin powder
- 1 cup fresh lime juice   6 banana leaves
- Habanero salsa   Fresh Pepper Pico (See veggies)

Layer the cubed pork (2in cube) on racks and cold-smoke with hickory for 2-3 hours, remove from box.

Line three disposable turkey roasting pans with 1 package of banana leaves leaving a overhang on all the edges. Layer the cubes of shoulder into the bottom of each.

Prepare the marinade by breaking the achiote bricks into pieces, and dropping them into a jar. Add the lime juice and 1 tablespoon of salt; blend until the mixture is a smooth, thickish, marinade.

Pour the achiote mixture over the pork, spreading it evenly to coat all surfaces (*You'll want to wear latex gloves, achiote will strain your hands red.*)

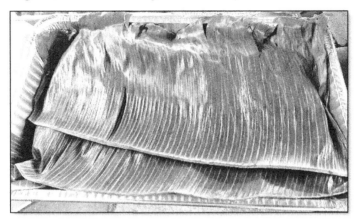

Fold the overhanging banana leaves over the pork, then use the last 3 banana leaves to cover the pork completely. Pour about 3 cups of water over the leaves—it will collect in the bottom of the pan and should be about 1 inch deep. Cover pan with foil.

Place the pans in the bottom of the Caja China, attach probe from the wired thermometer and run wire under short aluminum top frame. Start your smoker with **mesquite**, cover box with the ash pan and charcoal grid.

Add 16 lbs. of charcoal for Model #1 Box or 18lbs. for Model #2, or Semi Pro box, and light up. Once lit (20-25 minutes) spread the charcoal evenly over the charcoal grid. Cooking time starts right now. After 1 hour (1st hour) add 9 lbs. of charcoal (note time).

Continue to add 9 lbs. of charcoal every hour until you reach 195 F on the meat thermometer.

IMPORTANT: Do not open the box until you reach the desired temperature.

Once you reach 195 F, lift the charcoal grid shake it well to remove the ashes, now place it on top of the long handles. Do not place on the grass or floor - it will damage them. Remove the ash pan from the box and dispose of the ashes.

Remove the foil, cover the box again with the ash pan and the charcoal grid; do not add more charcoal at this time. After 30 minutes, take a peak by lifting the charcoal pan by one end only.

You will continue doing this every 10 minutes until the pork is crispy to your liking.

Remove the roasting pans (and pork) from the box, and toss the banana leaves. Test the fork-tender meat with an instant thermometer...it should be between 190 and 195 degrees.

Remove the meat, debone, and coarsely shred it into baking pans, and then slide all the meat, covered with foil, into a low oven, until you're ready to serve.

Pour the juices into a pan, and simmer until reduced by half, season with salt if needed.

Serve with meat on a deep platter with warm corn tortillas, black beans, and Pico de Gallo. (See recipe.)

Luau Pork Shoulders

While "babymooning" in Hawaii, my wife and I learned the island tradition of throwing a family luau in honor of a child's first birthday. In celebration of our daughter Grace, we hold this traditional feast each year.

4 - bnls pork shoulders (6lb ea)	4 C hot water
1 ½ gal Hawaiian Mojo	2 Tbs seasoned salt
½ C Stubbs liquid smoke	4 Tbs garlic powder
¼ C Adobo Criollo spices	6 Ti or banana leaves

Marinate pork in Hawaiian Mojo (*see recipe*) overnight.

Remove from marinade, pat dry, and inject each shoulder with 6-8ozs of remaining marinade.

Score pork on all sides, rub with salt, then brush with liquid smoke, and sprinkle with garlic.

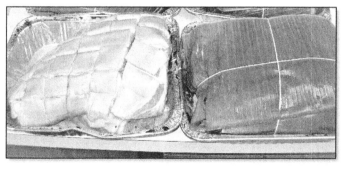

Wrap completely in Ti/Banana leaves, tie with string, and wrap in heavy foil

Place racks inside the box skin side down, attach probe from the wired thermometer and run wire under short aluminum top frame.

Start your smoker with **mesquite**, cover box with the ash pan and charcoal grid.

Add 16 lbs. of charcoal for Model #1 Box or 18lbs. for Model #2, or Semi Pro Box and light up. Once lit (20-25 minutes) spread the charcoal evenly over the charcoal grid. Cooking time starts right now. After 1 hour (1st hour) add 9 lbs. of charcoal (note time).

Continue to add 9 lbs. of charcoal every hour until you reach 195 F on the meat thermometer.

Once you reach 195 F, lift the charcoal grid shake it well to remove the ashes, now place it on top of the long handles. Do not place on the grass or floor - it will damage them.

IMPORTANT: Do not open the box until you reach the desired temperature.

Remove the ash pan from the box and dispose of the ashes.

Unwrap foil, peel back the banana leaves, and brush with mojo. Flip the pork shoulders over to crispy the skin.

This is easily done using the patented Rack System, just grab the end of the rack, and lift and slide as you pull upward, using the other hand grab the top end of the other rack and slide it down.

Score the skin using a knife, this helps to remove the fat and crisp the skin. Cover the box again with the ash pan and the charcoal grid; do not add more charcoal at th is time.

After 30 minutes, take a peek by lifting the charcoal pan by one end only. You will continue doing this every 10 minutes until the skin is crispy to your liking.

Remove shoulders from Caja and allow to rest 30 minutes.

Chop the meat and then mix with a wash of ½ cup liquid smoke, 4 cups hot water, ¼ cup Adobo Criollo spices, and 2 Tbs seasoned salt.

Let that sit about 15 minutes, drain remaining liquid, and serve with Sweet Hawaiian Pork Sauce (*see recipe.*)

Note: Traditionally this would be served with white or Hawaiian rice (see recipes.) A nice fruit salad in very complimentary as well.

If you really want to go "Big Island" serve this up with some Lomi-Lomi Salmon, Chicken Long Rice, and Pineapple Haupia. There are many wonderful Hawaiian cookbooks available, my favorite is *"Sam Choy's Sampler."*

Whole Hog BBQ

Of course, no book on La Caja China BBQ would be complete without including the reason the magic box was created in the first place, the amazing whole pig!

Below is the basic recipe, and then some various recipes and styles that can be used, using the same instructions.

Rinse the pig, inside and out, pat dry. Brush the pig down with baste and then rub all over with the seasoning and some fine sea salt. Put your pig in an ice filled cooler for 24-36 hours (*drain the water, and add ice as needed*).

The day you plan to cook, remove the pig from the cooler and let it warm up to room temperature. This is important for even cooking. Sprinkle the whole pig inside and out with fine sea-salt.

Position the roasting box is a safe, well ventilated area (*but out of direct drafts*). If roasting on the lawn, be sure to water the grass well before cooking, just in case.

Place 3-4 (*depending on size*) disposable drip pans in the bottom of the box, and add a couple of cups of water, apple juice, or beer to each pan. Remove one of the top end rails for ventilation.

Place the pig between the racks, belly up, and use the 4 S-Hooks to secure the two racks together, near the corners.

The rack legs should be facing away from the pig. Place the rack and pig into La Caja China.

Insert the probe from a wired thermometer into the thickest part of the pig's shoulder and run wire under the rail of the top frame.

Light your smoker unit (*pictured with the A-Maze-N Smoker*) with apple wood, and place it on top of the pig rack, over a small piece of foil to protect the bottom from moisture.

Close up the box with the ash pan, and charcoal grid, to cover.

Cover box with the ash pan and charcoal grid. Add 14 lbs. of charcoal for a 70# box or 16lbs of charcoal a 100# box, in two equal piles and light. Once lit (20-25 minutes) spread the charcoal evenly over the charcoal grid.

Add an additional 8 pounds of charcoal every hour until you reach 180 F on the meat thermometer (*7-8 hours*) keeping the box temp between 225F and 250F.

IMPORTANT: DON'T PEEK! Only lift the charcoal lid as instructed.

Lift the charcoal grid shake it well to remove the ashes, now place it on top of the La Caja China's long handles, or on two metal sawhorses. Do not place on the grass or asphalt! DO NOT Remove the ash pan from the box ~ Use a large metal scoop to dispose of the ashes.

Once you reach 195 F on your thermometer, repeat the steps to remove the ashes.

Open the box and remove the smoker. Flip the pig, skin-side up, salt and score the skin, by making an X in each square of the pig rack, using a very sharp knife. This helps to remove the fat and crisp the skin. Try to just cut the skin, and not into the meat.

Cover the box again with the ash pan and the charcoal grid; do not add more charcoal at this time.

After 30 minutes, take a peek by lifting the charcoal pan by one end only. You will continue doing this, every 10 minutes, until the skin is crispy to your liking.

Caja Tips:

When smoking with La Caja China, or Caja Asadora, leave the two end rails off the box for airflow (*this creates a ¼ inch gap at either end.*)

Set the smoker on a small piece of foil, directly on top of, and centered on, the pig rack.

Light the pellets with a torch, though a small hole in the end of the smoker. Do not use lighter fluid or any other accelerate to light.

Always position your smoker above meats, never below, to avoid being extinguished by drippings.

Never use a smoker in an enclosed area or without proper ventilation.

Carving a Whole BBQ Pig

One thing to keep in mind is that besides the bones, there is very little waste that comes from a whole pig. Some people even find the skin to be a delicacy.

Here are some guidelines on how you can approach it.

Having two people carve is ideal but if there will only be one person, then they should begin carving 15-20 minutes before the meal starts.

Make sure you have a sharp knife, tongs, a large fork, a pan to put the meat into and ample space.

You should carve the pig over roasting pans to catch the juices

You will start by carving half of the pig. Begin by removing half of the skin from the pig. I typically do one side, and then the other, but back to front works just as well. Doesn't really matter.

Start cutting at the neck and down along the spine. Then around the head to the bottom of the jaw and remove the skin.

With half of the skin removed, cut it into pieces for guests to enjoy. The other half of the pig should still have the skin on it till it is ready to be carved. This will help to keep in the heat while it's waiting.

The skin can be used to make pork rinds or used as flavoring for other dishes, But I usually chop them most of it and mix with the chopped meat from the rest of the pig. You can also leave the skin on, and chop it right along with the major cuts. Up to you.

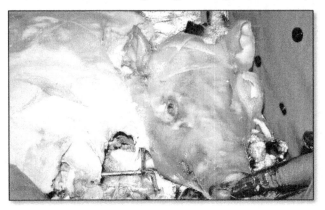

Next remove the head and front shoulders. Slice the meat from the bone in large pieces and set aside to chop. You want to wait to chop all of the meat together so that these first curs don't cool too much, or begin to dry, before you're done.

Note: *You may be squeamish, at first, about the head. But, as on most large animals (and large fish), the cheeks (or "jowls") contain some of the best tasting, unctuous meat on the entire animal. Don't waste it!*

Remove the back leg, carve the meat from the leg and slice into individual servings.

Then remove the back meat, pork loins and the meat along the spine.

Now you are left with the spare ribs. You can either remove them at this point or wait till the other half of the pig is carved.

If, like me, you don't want to waste a single bite, run a thin boning knife between each rib to remove the meat, and add it to the pan for chopping.

Once the ribs are removed, all that's really left on the spine in the tenderloins. They should be easily removeable by hand. Remove them, whole, and set aside with the rest.

Next, cut or pull the meat away from the bones of the hams and shoulders. Now, all of the meat should be off the bones, and you can chop it together for serving.

A couple of tips:

Adding hot juices from the drip pans, as you're mixing the chopped meat, will really add a punch of extra flavor, and keep it extra moist.

I add a little cider vinegar, a splash at a time, to the juices, for extra flavor.

Pork & Vinegar *are a classic combination. Not only does apple cider vinegar add a subtle tang, it also plays perfectly against the fattiness of the meat. Vinegar works as a palate-cleanser, as well, keeping the taste-buds for getting saturated with fat, so the flavors of each bite are as vibrant as the first.*

Once your pig is all chopped, and the juices have been added, allow it to rest for 10-15 minutes for the meat to absorb, and then taste for seasoning.

Add a little salt and/or black pepper here, to perfect the flavor before serving.

I like to have two chafing pans set up (over simmering water), one to hold the whole cuts, and one to add the chopped meat to.

This helps keeps the meat tender and at safe temps until your guests dig in.

Don't forget! *We covered the basics of injecting whole pigs, as well as three of my favorite injection recipes, back in* **Chapter Three: Techniques.**

More Whole Hog Options

Filipino Lechon

In the Philippines, pig roast is also called "lechon." The cooked pig is often served with an apple in its mouth. "Lechon" is a must at all holiday parties and celebrations like anniversaries, christenings, birthdays.

And, ask most Filipino's where to find the best pig, and they'll send you to the small town of Cebu, which was colonized by the Spanish more than 400 years ago (*and the Spanish, of course, brought pigs.*) Cebu's lechon is so wildly popular in the Philippines, that domestic airlines accept it as regular freight, straight from the spit to all parts of the country!

Now, that's a body-cavity search I could get behind!

Cebu Lechon

- 1 (*45- to 50-pound*) dressed pig
- soy sauce
- salt and black pepper to taste

Marinade:

- 2 liters of Sprite or 7up
- 1 liter of coconut water

Stuffing:

10 bundles lemon grass	6 bay leaves (*crumbled*)
4 lbs green onion (*greens*)	¼ cup star anise
5 cups of crushed garlic	2 quartered saba bananas

Marinate the pig (*chilled*), skin side down, overnight in 2-3 inches of Sprite and coconut water, sprinkled with salt.

Before roasting, bring the pig to room temp (*discard the marinade.*)

Par-cook the bananas by boiling 5 minutes.

Rub the whole pig with salt and pepper, the brush the cavity with soy sauce.

Pack the belly cavity with saba bananas, anise, green onion leaves, crushed garlic and bay. Stack on the lemon grass, and cover just the belly cavity with foil.

Bring pig to room temperature before roasting, and place 3 large disposable steam pans under the bottom rack in your La Caja China, to catch the juices.

Follow the La Caja Cooking Instructions on pages 131-139

After flipping the pig, brush the skin side generously with more of the Sprite/Coconut mixture, before crisping.

Strain the broth from the pans, and serve the pig with sticky rice, and hot broth on the side.

For an even more traditional version, use the Pig, Hog, and Lamb Rotisserie for the Caja China Box.

Rotisserie Instructions:

- Do not marinate the pig in advance, nor do you want to butterfly the carcass, as in box roasting. Stuff the marinade into the cavity, sew closed with wet kitchen string, and use the marinade to brush the exterior of the pig, while it roasts over the coals.

- Do not set up your coals directly under the pig, place disposable steam pans in the center on the grill, and run two rows of coals down either side, the length of the pig.

Don't worry about kids "freaking out" at the sight of a whole pig. In my experience, children are WAY more curious about the "new & unusual" than adults!

Hawaiian Kālua Pua'a

The Hawaiian method of cooking whole hogs in a pit hearkens back to their Polynesian culture.

The centerpiece of any Hawaiian celebration is the *Kālua Pua'a* (whole roast pig), typically served with, rice, fresh fruit, sweet potatoes, poi (pounded taro root) and any number of local seafood dishes like lau lau, lomi salmon, and squid luau. The word kālua literally means "to cook in an underground oven", which of course, makes it a perfect recipe for your La Caja China.

Done right, the Pua'a meat falls off the bone, and is typically very tender and moist, with a slightly salty, smoky flavor that is incomparable with any other style of pig.

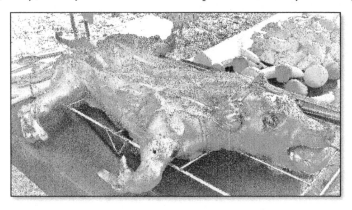

Kālua Pua'a

- 40-45lb pig, cleaned and butterflied
- 2lb coarse sea salt
- Banana leaves, soaked in water*

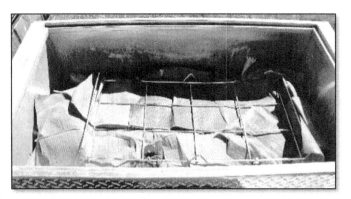

Line the bottom roasting box with a double layer of banana leaves, then set the pig down on top of the rack, skin side up. Coat the pig half of the salt, flip *(just the pig)* and coat the belly side with the remaining salt.

Cover the pig with another layer of banana leaves, and secure the rack.

Fill and light your smoker with mesquite, and place it on the center of the top rack (*remember to remove the end rails of your box, to allow for air.*)

Follow the La Caja Cooking Instructions on pages 131-139

Plan to <u>double the roasting time</u>, to achieve the fall-apart texture of real Kālua Pua'a. Once you've flipped the pig, (**removing the foil, and all of the banana leaves**), scored the skin, and continue with the basic instructions.

Noho me ka hau'oli!
(Be happy!)

*Banana leaves can often be found in the frozen produce section or grocery stores, or check out any local Polynesian or Asian stores. If you can't find them anywhere local, you can order them online.

Soak the banana leave in hot water for an hour, to make them pliable, and keep them from scorching too much, while roasting.

Cuban Lechon Asado

Then, of course, there's Cuba, motherland of the magic box.

In Cuba, roasting a whole pig is the main event and most anticipated course in holiday parties, especially Christmas and New Year. For Noche Buena (*Christmas Eve*) families gather together as a time for rekindling of ties among families as they celebrate the coming of Christmas. A Cuban feast just wouldn't be complete without the roasted pig. The hogs are marinated in sour orange juice, garlic, oregano, and salt, a combination called Mojo (*mo-ho*).

The feast typically includes black beans, white rice, tostones (*fried plantains*), yuca con mojo, salad and lots of Cuban bread

Lechon Asado

- 1 (45- to 50-pound) dressed pig
- 1/3 cup Adobo Criollo
- 2 cups coarse sea salt

Mojo

Note: Sour oranges can be hard to find outside of Cuba and Florida, this recipe creates a similar flavor by combining both sweet and sour citrus.

- 5 heads garlic, peeled   1 tsp. black peppercorns
- 3 cup fresh orange juice   2 ½ tsp. oregano
- 1 tsp. ground bay leaves   2 ½ tsp. coarse sea salt
- 1 ½ cups fresh lemon juice   1 scotch bonnet pepper (opt.)

For every head of peeled garlic cloves, add ½ teaspoon salt, six black peppercorns, and ½ teaspoon of oregano.

Mash this combination into a paste with a mortar and pestle (*or food processor*). Scoop the paste into another bowl.

For every head of peeled garlic cloves, add ½ teaspoon salt, six black peppercorns, and ½ teaspoon of oregano. Mash this combination into a paste with a mortar and pestle ( ). Scoop the paste into another bowl.

Repeat the process until you've used up all of the garlic. If adding the scotch bonnet pepper, grind it with the last batch (carefully), and then whisk the whole bowl to combine.

Combine the orange juice and lemon juice, and let sit at room temperature for an hour.

Use immediately to marinate the pig, or refrigerate is using later.

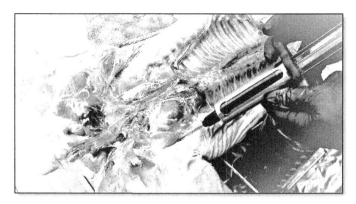

Place pig skin side down on a large table. Strain ¼ of the mojo into tall glass, reserving the solids. Transfer liquid to a large syringe and inject into the meat of the pig every 3 to 4 inches, on a grid, (*be careful in the thinner sections, not to push the needle all the way through the meat.*)

Sprinkle both sides of the pig with coarse sea salt, and adobo criollo and rub it in well; use the reserved solids from mojo to coat the body cavity. Cover, and chill the whole pig overnight.

Bring pig to room temperature before roasting, and place 3 large disposable steam pans under the bottom rack in your La Caja China, to catch the juices.

Follow the La Caja Cooking Instructions on pages 131-138

Heat juices from the pans, strain, and transfer to a serving bowl.

Serve meat on rolls topped with warm mojo and chopped onions.

Delicioso!

When a customer asks for a "head-off" presentation, my favorite sous chef and I save them to roast for tacos!

Poultry

The Basics of Brining

In cooking, brining is a process similar to marinating, in which meat is soaked in brine before cooking.

Brining makes cooked meat moister by hydrating the cells of its muscle tissue before cooking, via the process of osmosis, and by allowing the cells to hold on to the water while they are cooked, via the process of denaturation.

How long to brine depends on the size and type of meat you've got. Larger meats like a whole turkey need more time for the brine to do its magic. Small pieces of seafood like shrimp shouldn't sit in a brine for more than half an hour, or so.

Fatty meats like beef and lamb are generally not improved by brining.

My basic brine = *1 cup coarse sea salt + 1 cup sugar (white or brown) + 1 gallon purified water.*

Bring water to a high simmer, add salt and sugar to dissolve, and allow to cool to room temp before adding the meat. You can increase or decrease the amount of brine, as long as you have enough to completely submerse the meat, by modifying the brine ingredients in these proportions. How much brine do you need?

Here's a tip: put your meat in the container you're going to soak it in, then fill it with purified water until completely covered. Remove the meat, and then use this water to make your brine. Clever, huh? One caveat with brining is that whatever you put the meat in, needs to fit in your refrigerator or cooler. Both the meat and brine need to stay below 40F at all times.

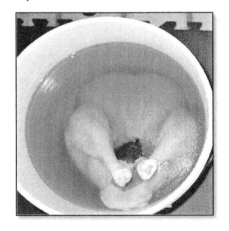

This isn't a big deal with a couple of pork chops, but can present some logistical headaches when you're roasting half-a - dozen turkeys, as I do each

Thanksgiving. In this case, your best bet is to sterilize a cooler that's big enough to fit the meat, brine, and a couple of bags of ice.

General Brining Times

Whole Chicken ~ 4 to 12 hours

Chicken legs, wings & thighs ~ 1 to 1 ½ hours

Whole Turkey ~ 24 hours

Turkey Breast ~ 5 to 8 hours

Cornish Game Hens ~ 1 to 2 hours

The beauty of a good brine is you can add whatever you want to it!

I often add quartered lemons and chopped garlic to my whole chicken brine, and Chinese 5 Spice to my pork brine. The best flavored brines are often the simplest...citrus juice and dried mint will add a nice Mediterranean flavor to chicken, while cracked black pepper and red wine vinegar provide a rich French flair.

After brining, always rinse your meat and dry it well before cooking. Otherwise, your dinner is going to be super salty

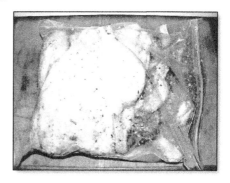

Likewise, don't salt the brined meat before, during, or after cooking, nor any sauces or gravies you make with the residual broth (*which is...awesome!*)

Stock from brined poultry may require some diluting with water, or better yet milk.

Lastly, make sure to keep a close eye when cooking meats that have been brined. Brining adds sugar to the meat and can cause it to burn faster.

4 Tips for the Perfect La Caja China Turkey

Every year, I roast 8-10 whole turkeys in our Semi Pro for the Thanksgiving dinner at our local homeless shelter, The Father's Heart, in Oregon City.

Here are 5 tips we've learned over the years, for roasting the perfect turkey(s) in La Caja China roasting boxes.

THAW

Make sure your turkey(s) are COMPLETELY thawed by the night before.

The bone temp of the turkeys will make or break the La Caja China process. The USDA recommends cold water thawing.

Allow about 30 minutes per pound, and be sure the turkey is in a leak-proof plastic bag to prevent cross-contamination and to prevent the turkey from absorbing water, resulting in a watery product.

Submerge the wrapped turkey in cold tap water. Change the water every 30 minutes until the turkey is thawed. Cook the turkey immediately after it is thawed.

FOIL

Just Also, be sure to cover (just) the top of each turkey loosely with a small piece of foil.

The thin skin burns easily in the direct heat of the roasting box lid.

You need a separate piece for each turkey, so you don't block the heat getting down and under the birds *(been there, done that!)*

NO PEEKING

I know I'm a bit of a broken record on this subject, but it really is important. Lifting the lid from the box effectively removes all the cooking heat, and it takes a LONG time to build back up, as your turkey is cooling at the same time. Use a remote probe thermometer in the thickest part of the thigh, and *(personal opinion)* a metal dust pan and scoop to remove the ashes, instead of removing the lid.

COLD WEATHER

Let's face it, holiday cooking, for many of us, means if we want to BBQ or grill…we're cooking in the cold! Make sure you start out with every ounce of the recommended coal weight, to ensure that the box reaches its "honey spot" for you.

Keeping the box protected from the wind is key, I often start mine in the driveway, and once the fire had gone out, roll it into my garage – keeping the door open, and the box a safe distance from any flammables, of course!

Also, shave 10 minutes of each "add coals" cycle; this has helped me in the past.

My Best Brined Turkey Recipe

I gotta say, if given a choice I will never, NEVER serve another turkey (*or chicken*) that has not been brined. The improvement in moistness, flavor, and general "cook-ability" makes it a no-brainer. The aromatics make a huge difference as well. My wife had made it clear that the testing is over, THIS is our Thanksgiving turkey recipe from now on, and no modifications are allowed!

Per each (*14 to 16 pound*) frozen young turkey:

For the brine:

- 1 cup kosher salt
- 1 quart turkey stock
- 2 Tbs. black pepper
- 1 gallon heavily iced water
- 1 cup of honey
- 1 quart boiling water
- 1 ½ tsp. chopped candied ginger

For the aromatics:

- 1 red apple, sliced
- 1 onion, sliced
- 1 cup water
- 6 leaves sage
- 2 med pears, sliced
- 1 cinnamon stick
- 4 sprigs rosemary
- Canola oil

2 to 3 days before roasting:

Begin thawing the turkey in the refrigerator or in a cooler kept at 38F.

Combine the stock, water, salt, honey, peppercorns, and candied ginger in a large stockpot over medium-high heat. Stir occasionally to dissolve solids and bring to a boil. Remove the brine from the heat, cool to room temperature, and refrigerate.

Early on the day or the night before you'd like to eat:

Combine the brine, water and ice in the 5-gallon bucket, or cooler(s).

Place the thawed turkey (with innards removed) breast side down in brine.

If necessary, weigh down the bird to ensure it is fully immersed, cover, and refrigerate or set in cool area for 8 to 16 hours, turning the bird once half way through brining.

Remove the bird from brine and rinse inside and out with cold water. Discard the brine. Place the bird on roasting rack, breast up, and pat dry with paper towels.

Combine the apple, pears, onion, cinnamon stick, and 1 cup of water in a microwave safe dish and microwave on high for 5 minutes.

Add steeped aromatics to the turkey's cavity along with the rosemary and sage. Tuck the wings underneath the bird and coat the skin liberally with canola oil.

Cook as instructed above.

Caja Smoked Turkey

- 1 (10 lb.) whole turkey
- 2 tablespoons sea salt
- 2 cans Dr. Pepper
- 1 onion, quartered
- 1 tablespoon salt

4 cloves garlic, crushed
½ cup butter
1 apple, quartered
1 Tbs. garlic powder
1 Tbs. ground black pepper

Directions

Preheat the box to 225-250F

Rinse turkey *(neck and giblets removed)* with cold water, and pat dry. Rub the crushed garlic over the outside of the bird, and sprinkle with seasoned salt. Place, on end, in a disposable roasting pan.

Fill turkey cavity with butter, cola, apple, onion, garlic powder, salt, and ground black pepper, and lay down breast up. Cover loosely in foil, with several pencil-sized holes poked in it.

Smoke for 8 hours with mesquite, uncover, and smoke an additional 2 hours, or until internal temperature reaches 180F *(measured in the thickest part of the thigh.)*

Baste the bird every 30 minutes during these last 2 hours with the juices from the bottom of the roasting pan.

Remove turkey (and pan) from the box, flip the turkey breast-down, and let rest 30 minutes, tented loosely in foil.

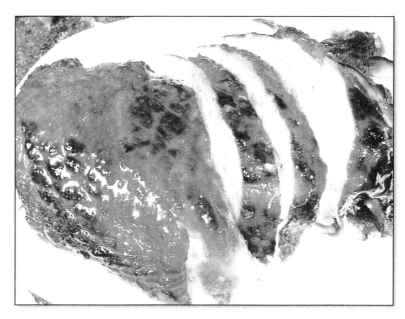

Perfect Smoked Turkey Breast

Cooking a whole, bone-in smoked turkey breast is a great option if you don't want to smoke a whole turkey. And if you prefer white meat, you've got it made, since the breast is 100% white.

After brining, pat the turkey breasts dry with a towel and allow to air-dry at room temperature while the smoker heats up.

Preheat your roasting box to 325F. I recommend hickory.

Apple wood smoke has a light flavor and produces a nice color on on poultry.

Do not add a water pan for this recipe, as the moisture inhibits the turkey skin from browning nicely.

Smoke to an internal temperature of 160F.

Remove, tent with foil, and rest 15 minutes before slicing and serving.

Tom Tom Turkey Drumsticks

Smoked drumsticks are…awesome!

Brine with 1 Tbs. of kosher salt, and 1 Tbs. brown sugar per cup of water.

You need enough brine to cover the legs so how much you need depends on the size of container you are using. An easy way to figure it out is to place the turkey legs in a container and pour in the water a cup at a time until they are covered. This will tell you how much brine to prepare.

After brining 6-8 hours, rinse well and drain.

Dry them off with paper towels to ready them for the dry rub.

Photo by Nim Garcia

Season each leg with a couple of teaspoons of the dry rub, and smoke them at 250 with apple, or cherry, for 4-6 hours, or to 180F.

When done, let rest for half an hour before serving. Leftovers make amazing sandwiches!

Tom Tom Rub

- 2 Tbs. onion powder
- 2 Tbs. sweet paprika
- 1 Tbs. coarse ground black pepper
- 1 tsp. garlic powder

Slow-Smoked Apple Chicken

Smoking a chicken is easy and amazing!

Per Chicken:

- 1 3-4lb chicken
- 1 Tbs. smoked paprika
- 1 Tbs. garlic powder
- 2 Tbs. chili powder

¼ cup brown sugar, packed
1 Tbs. onion powder
1 Tbs. oregano
1 tsp. seasoned salt

Remove giblets from your chicken, and run cold water over your chicken and rinse well. Pat dry, and put chicken in a pan.

In a small bowl, mix all the dry rub ingredients listed above. Generously rub the chicken all over until the rub is gone.

Place plastic wrap over the pan and refrigerate overnight. (At least 8 to 12 hours.) After the chicken has marinated, turn on your smoker (or light it) and preheat the box to 225F.

Once preheated, place the whole chicken on the rack breast side up and close you're the box.

Smoke the chicken at a box temp of 225F for about 4 to 5 hours. Do not let it get over 250F.

After 4 hours, insert a digital thermometer into the thickest part of the thigh, and continue smoking until the chicken reaches 165F.

Remove the chicken. Breasts should be at 165F and the thighs/legs 175F.

Let the chicken rest for 10-15 minutes before cutting and serving.

Smoked Chicken Thighs

Chicken thighs are the most forgiving cut on the bird, with enough fat to keep them moist for just about any form of cooking, and making them ideal for BBQ and grilling.

I prefer to use bone-in, as the bone adds more flavor to the meat while cooking.

- 8 – bone-in chicken thighs
- 1 tsp oregano
- 1 tsp dried thyme
- 1 tsp lemon pepper
- ¼ tsp Mexican chili powder

2 tsp brown sugar
1 tsp dried basil
1 tsp onion powder
½ tsp garlic powder
½ cup butter, melted

Mix spices and herbs. Rub all side of the thighs, including the skin, and let rest 2-3 hours, covered in foil.

Smoke, skin-side up, at a box temp of 250F, using hickory. At one hour flip the thighs.

After two hours, start checking the temps, smoking until they reach 180 degrees (*2-3 hours, depending on the size of the thighs.*)

Remove thighs from smoker, and let rest 10 minutes, tented in foil, the brush with melted butter, and serve.

Smoked Chicken Taquitos

- 16 corn tortillas
- 2 cups melted lard
- 8 ounces shredded queso
- ½ cup chili verde sauce
- 16 toothpicks

6 Smoked Chicken Thighs
¼ cup Mexican cream
1 cup guacamole sauce
1 cup shredded cilantro
Crema (*Mexican Sour Cream*)

Debone and shred the smoked chicken thighs.

Add 1 tablespoon of shredded chicken, and 2 tsp. shredded queso fresco for each warmed corn tortilla. Roll up and pin with a toothpick.

Fry them in ½ inch of lard, over medium heat, turning them once. Should be well browned on both sides.

Drain the cooked taquitos on napkins or paper towels to remove excess oil so that they are not overly greasy.

Assembling the Dish

Place four cooked taquitos on a plate.
Spread a teaspoon of cream on each one.
Spread a Tbs. of avocado salsa on each one, then ½ Tbs of salsa verde.
Sprinkle with shredded queso fresco, crema, and cilantro.

Avocado Salsa

- 2 very ripe avocados
- 6 sprigs of cilantro
- 1 clove garlic
- 1 tsp. salt

3 small tomatillos
1/4 white onion
Juice of 2 limes

Combine ingredients and puree until smooth.

Smokey Mojo Chicken

A flattened, or "spatchcocked" chicken cooks in less time than a regular chicken and can be grilled or roasted without becoming overcooked. Mojo [MOH-hoh] is considered the signature marinade of Cuba, and is used to complement a wide variety of foods such as beef, pork and poultry.

- 6 - 4lb whole chickens
- 12 C Traditional Cuban Mojo
- 6 Tbs Adobo Criollo spice blend

6 Tbs olive oil
6 tsp sea salt

Rinse chicken with cold water and pat dry. Cut out backbone with kitchen shears.

For more details on spatchcocking a whole chicken, be sure tto watch my video at **www.cajachinavideos.com**

Turn chicken breast side up and open like a book. Press down firmly on breast to flatten and break rib bones. Loosen skin from body under breast and thighs.

Place each chicken in a gallon-size resealable bag with 2 cups Mojo. Marinate (flat) in refrigerator 24 hours.

Remove chickens from bags and discard mojo. Blot each bird dry, and rub each with 1 Tbs olive oil, and then 1 Tbs. Adobo Criollo spice blend.

Cold smoke chicken in La Caja China for 1 hour, on racks, using apple wood.

Place chickens (*flattened*) breast up on a roasting pan with a rack, and sprinkle with salt. Flip and repeat. Add a couple of cups of warm water to each pan, and tent each chicken loosely with foil.

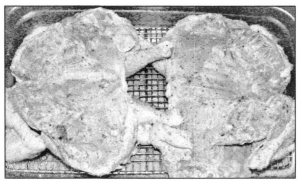

Using one of the center chickens, insert a thermometer probe into the thickest part of a thigh, but not touching the bone. Add 12 lbs. of charcoal for model #1 or 15 lbs. for model #2 or Semi Pro Box, and light up. Once lit (20-25 minutes) spread the charcoal evenly over the charcoal grid.

Cook to 170F (about 1 hour), remove foil, flip and roast, if necessary 5-10 more minutes to brown. Remove chickens from La Caja China, and allow to rest for 5 minutes. Halve, quarter, or carve the chicken and serve with Quick Saffron Basmati Rice.

IMPORTANT: Do not open the box until you reach the desired temperature.

Both Cuban Mojo and Authentic Cuban Adobo Criollo can be purchased directly from La Caja China at www.shoplatintouch.com (under "Accessories.")

La Caja China Smoked Christmas Goose

Roast goose is a favorite Christmas dish in Sweden (as well as many other countries.) Goose is very different than turkey, as the meat is dark and roasts up like a lean roast beef. A bonus with roast goose is its crispy skin, second only to pig skin…it's the best!

- 8 to 10 lb goose
- 2 onions, cut into wedges
- 1 lemon, halved
- 3 cups chicken stock

Salt and pepper to taste
¼ cup flour
4 to 6 apples, cut into wedges
Salt and pepper -- to season

The typical goose serves just 4 to 6 people, so for large parties, roast two or more.

Remove the goose from the refrigerator about 45 minutes before you start cooking, and let it come to room temperature.

Wash the goose with cold water, pat it dry with paper towels and tuck the wings under the body to keep them from burning. Prick the goose skin all over with a skewer or toothpick. Trim any excess fat from the opening of the body cavity.

One way to get the skin really crispy is by dipping the bird (raw) into boiling water for about 30 seconds. Rinse with cold water, pat dry and refrigerate 2 days. This tightens up and dries the skin, making it crisper in the end.

Rub the goose with the lemon and season the inside and outside of the bird liberally with salt and pepper.

Stuff the chopped apples and onions into the body cavity. Set the goose, breast side down, on a rack in La Caja China's roasting pan.

Instructions for Model #3:

Place tray with meat inside the box, cover box with the ash pan, add 5 lbs. of charcoal and light up. Set up smoker with pecan wood.

Once lit (20-25 minutes) spread the charcoal evenly over the tray.

Meanwhile, add the reserved giblets (minus the liver), neckbone and 3 cups of water or stock to a medium saucepan. Bring to a boil, then reduce heat to low and simmer while you finish roasting the goose and preparing the rest of your dinner. Add water or stock as necessary to keep the amount of liquid around 3 cups.

After 1 hour of roasting open the box, carefully turn the goose over so it is breast side up and prick the skin all over again. Baste the goose again, connect the wired thermometer probe in the thickest part of the goose thigh, tent goose with foil. close the box and add 4 lbs. of charcoal.

After 1 hour (2nd hour) to add 6 lbs. of charcoal cook for 30-45 minutes, until the temperature in the thickest part of the thigh measures between 165°F and 175°F.

Remove foil to brown the bird and check every couple of minutes until browned to your liking.

Remove the goose from La Caja China, tent with foil and let it rest for at least 15 minutes while you make the gravy.

Strain the simmering stock. Pour any excess fat out of the roasting pan (*there will be a lot*), leaving about 4 tablespoons in the pan.

Don't throw away that goose fat! It's as good as bacon fat for sautéing potatoes and vegetables!

Place the pan over a medium-low flame on the stovetop and whisk the flour into the fat. Let the flour cook and bubble for a minute or two until it turns a light golden brown.

Whisk in the goose stock, scraping the bits of drippings off the pan.

Let the goose gravy simmer and thicken for about 5 to 7 minutes. Season with salt and pepper and strain into a gravy boat.

To carve, first remove the wings, then the legs. Cut the legs into drumsticks and thighs. Then cut down each side of breast and carve each breast into thin slices.

This recipe can be tripled, or quadrupled for La Caja China models #1, #2, and Semi-Pro by simply multiplying all of the ingredients by 3 or 4.

Start the roasting box with 15lbs of charcoal, and add 10lbs ever hour, according to recipe instructions. Cook times may vary, so be sure to use a probe thermometer to track the temperature in the thickest part of the meat.

Merry Christmas!

FISH & SEAFOOD

Our early ancestors were "smoking" meat for as long as they had access to meat and smoke, to avoid spoilage and preserve food for the lean seasons.

Coastal Stone Age pe oples had a huge variety fish and seafood, and smoking was the preferred method of preserving their catches. The surplus was traded with other groups far inland for other necessities, uniting isolated communities, some of whom would never see the ocean, and forming the earliest trade routes.

In Medieval Europe most communities had smoke houses where meat could be smoked and stored.

Smaller and poorer communities would hang their fish high up in fireplaces, or in the rafters of the lodge-houses of my own Pacific Northwest ancestors, where the smoke from their hearth fires collected.

Early smoking methods of the Caribbean Islands natives, using high racks over low smoky fires even led to the cooking styles that we currently think of as grilling and BBQ.

It can be argued that the ability y to smoke meat, especially fish, was a key component in the age of discovery, allowing sea-faring ships to feed their crews during those long ocean voyages of discovery and trade.

To this day the smoking of fish and sea-food is carried out around the world and little has changed in the process and unique flavors of smoked salmon, trout, haddock, codfish, and innumerable other species. Flavors that our earliest ancestors would have recognized and savored as much as we do today.

How to remove pin-bones from salmon

As we're going to have a number of delectable salmon recipes in this book, I thought we should cover one of the most frequently asked questions when dealing with these most perfect of all fishes.

"What's up with all those freakin' little bones down the center of the salmon fillet I just bought?"

Those pesky bones are called "pin bones" — or "intermuscular bones" when you're hanging with your zoologist pals — and they're found in many popular fish, especially salmon. There are, on average, 16 pin-bones in each salmon fillet.

Lay the fillet flat on a work surface and feel along the upper half of the salmon with your thumb, and you will feel these bones. Without removing them, the finished fillet will be unpleasant, even dangerous, to eat.

As you find each pin-bone, put your hand under the fillet (*beneath that bone*) and lift it slightly until the bone protrudes. (*You can also lay the fillet over an inverted bowl, to do the same thing.*)

Grasp the end of the bone with fish tweezers or needle-nose pliers and pull it slowly out at the same angle it's in (so as not to tear the flesh) and wiggle it gently until it pulls free. Repeat for each pin-bone.

Chef's Chris' Fire Camp Salmon

In September of 2017, Chef Chris Renner and I spent two weeks as volunteers, feeding volunteers, evacuees, and fire-fighters of the Eagle Creek forest fires. One of the local native fisherman generously donated several beautiful, fresh from the river, and we wanted to cook them up the same day, with ingredients we had on hand.

That's how this recipe was born, and it's still one of the best ways to serve salmon that I've ever had!

- 1 lg fresh salmon fillet   ½ Cup of Yoshida's Original
- ½ Cup light brown sugar   ½ Cup grape jelly (*seriously*)
- 1 cup sweet cream butter   2 Tbs. coarse sea salt

Remove any pin-bones from your fillet and slice into 3-4 inch wide steaks. Melt butter, and keep warm.

Combine Yoshida sauce, brown sugar, and grape jelly in a saucepan, and warm to just steaming, whisking to combine. Remove sauce from heat. Brush the steaks with butter, salt lightly, and hot smoke at a box temp of 375 for 15 minutes, using Alder smoke.

Move steaks to a disposable pan, brush generously with half of the sauce, and smoke 10 more minutes, brushing with remaining sauce halfway through.

Remove salmon from the box and let rest 5 minutes before serving, with steamed rice.

Optional: Finish by charring lightly under broiler.

Smokey Dill Lemon Salmon

This heavy, flavorful fish is named for the Chinook Indians - master traders and fishermen who are now almost gone from the face of the earth, but once enjoyed a peaceful existence along the Columbia River and Northwest Coast.

1 - 6lb Chinook salmon fillets	Salt to taste
½ C butter, melted	½ C lemon juice
2 Tbs dried dill weed	2 tsp. garlic salt
Black pepper to taste	2 C plain yogurt

Cold smoke the filet, on a grate, with alder wood, for 2 hours.

Place salmon in a baking dish. Mix the butter and ½ lemon juice in a small bowl, and drizzle over the salmon. Season with salt & pepper.

Combine yogurt, dill, garlic powder, sea salt, and pepper.

Spread ½ of the sauce evenly over salmon. Return the salmon, on folded piece of foil, to the rack, add a chimney full of coals, and smoke at a box temp of 350F for 30-40 minutes, until fish flakes evenly.

Plate and spoon extra sauce over.

Henry Childs Gravlax & Nova Lox

"If you cold smoke it...best salmon you've ever had!" ~ *Henry*

- 1 cup Morton's Kosher Salt   1 cup white sugar
- 1 tsp. coarse black pepper   1 tsp. white pepper
- 2 sprigs of fresh dill, chopped   ¼ cup vodka
- zest of 1 lime

Remove pin-bones from the fillet. Put the salmon a shallow dish and pour the vodka over it. Sprinkle with white and black pepper, lime zest, and chopped dill.

Mix salt and sugar thoroughly.

Spread 1/3 of the cure over the bottom of a glass baking dish, just large enough to hold the fillet.

Place the fillet on top of the cure (*make sure the cure extends 1/2 inch past the edges of the salmon on all sides.*)

Spread the remaining 2/3 of the cure over the top to cover the fillet completely.

Cover the pan with plastic wrap and cure 5-7 days in the refrigerator. It will be cured and edible at this point.

After curing, rinse the fillet thoroughly, pat dry. Arrange it skin down on a wire rack over a sheet pan, and let it dry, uncovered, in the refrigerator until it feels tacky (*about 4 hours.*)

What you have now is called "Gravlax."

The difference between gravlax and nova lox, is to now add smoke:

Place salmon (*and rack*) it in the bottom of the box, over a foil-covered pan.

Cold smoke with alder until the exterior is a deep bronze color, and feels semi-firm and leathery (*about 8 hours.*)

Wrap the fillet in butcher paper and let it rest in the refrigerator for at least 4-6 hours, or overnight.

Serve in paper-thin slices, cut on the diagonal.

Uncle Art's Huckleberry Sweet Wine Salmon

Brine:

- 1 gallon of water, hot
- 2 C brown sugar
- 1 C huckleberries, pureed

1 C fine sea salt
2 Tbs. of molasses

Baste:

- 1 C sweet red wine

Combine the water, salt, sugar, molasses and pureed huckleberries. Whisk until sugar and salt are combine and allow to cool. Brine fillet 24 hours in refrigerator, then rinse well in cold water. Pat dry, and return to fridge, uncovered, 2-4 hours to dry the surface.

"The huckleberries will make the outside appear black, once smoked, and that distinctive Huck flavor is enhanced in a smoker." ~ Uncle Art

Start Caja China with one chimney of coals. When coals are gray, spread them down the center of the grate.

Place the fillet in the box, on a wire grate over a drip pan. Brush with ½ of the wine, close the box, and cold smoke with apple wood for 2 hours.

Cold smoke the filet, on a grate, with alder wood, for 2 hours.

After 2 hours, baste the fillet with the remaining wine, add two chimneys full of coals, and smoke at 350F for 30-40 minutes, until fish flakes evenly. (*Watch fillet closely and cover any hotspots with foil.*)

Plate and spoon pan drippings over the top.

Smokey Sweet-Soy Cedar Plank Salmon

I love salmon, especially our local Pacific salmon. When shopping for salmon look for fillets that say "no color added", and preferably "never frozen". Some meats can hold up to the cell-busting process of freezing and thawing…but salmon's not one of them.

This recipe, served over some lightly-salted Jasmine rice might be the best salmon dish I've ever had.

Add a little color with a fresh steamed green veggie like broccoli or green beans.

- 4 (6-oz) Pacific salmon fillets   1 Tbsp fine sea salt
- ½ tsp ground black pepper   1 C Sweet Soy Glaze
- ¼ C Melted butter   Extra-virgin olive oil
- 2 untreated cedar grilling planks*   Squirt bottle of water (*opt*)

Soak cedar grilling planks (*available on the bbq aisle, or online*) in enough water to cover for 2 hours, keep them immersed. Remove, pat dry with paper towels.

Prepare your grill for direct-heat cooking over medium-hot charcoal (*medium-high heat for gas*). Place the cedar planks over the heat. Brush skin-side of salmon with oil.

When planks begins to smoke, place salmon on the plank, skin side down (*if salmon is too wide for plank, fold in thinner side under to fit*) and salt lightly. If planks catch fire, spray the hot spots lightly with water. Brush salmon with sweet-soy glaze.

Grill, covered with lid, until salmon is just cooked through and edges are browned, 13 to 15 minutes.

Let salmon stand on plank 5 minutes before serving.

Serve with Jasmine rice and a steamed green veggie.

Smoked Honey Swai/Tilapia

Swai is a species native to the rivers of Southeast Asia, also known as iridescent shark. It's not a shark, but rather a catfish.

It is found in the Mekong basin as well as the Chao Phraya River, and is heavily cultivated for food there. The meat is often marketed under the common name swai. The meat is beige color when raw, and turns white after cooking.

In the U.S. it is often sold as frozen skin-off fillets weighing from 2 oz to 11 oz each.

In my opinion it's similar to Tilapia, but more flavorful.

I just happened to have a case of these lovelies in my freezer when my last roasting box arrived. Any of the larger model boxes can easily smoke 3 dozen fillets at a time, and that if you layer your racks with spacers.

Here's a simple, inexpensive, and delicious meal for my fellow fish fanciers…

Caja Smoked Honey Swai or Tilapia

- 2-3 lbs. swai or tilapia fillets
- 4 cups water
- 2/3 cup brown sugar
- Granulated garlic
- Apple or alder Traeger pellets

½ – ¾ cup clover honey
¼ cup sea salt
Black pepper
Cayenne (opt)

Thaw and rinse the fillets.

For brine: Combine water, sea salt, and brown sugar. Whisk to dissolve and pour over fish fillets (I put it all in a gallon zip bag) and brine for 1 hour.

To Cook

Remove fish from brine, rinse in cold water and pat dry, and then generously glaze each fillet with honey (*top side only.*)

Sprinkle with pepper, granulated garlic, and cayenne to taste.

Loaded fillets onto racks and place in the bottom of the box over foil-lined pans.

Smoke 20 minutes with apple wood, at a box temp of 225F for 40 minutes.

DO NOT PEEK! Remove swai from the box and serve.

I like to place mine directly over a bed of white rice, and let rest for about 10 minutes, so the juices from the fish seep into the rice, then serve with a steamed veggie. See top picture.

The leftover swai (*assuming you have any*) is great the next morning, chopped and scrambled with eggs and white onions, and served with hot white-corn tortillas!

Hot or Cold Smoked Trout

I have smoked a LOT of trout, since I drown my first worm as a wee lad, and I've tried just about every recipe I could find and, after four decades, I've come to the conclusion that simple is best.

The mild flavor of trout is quickly overwhelmed with much more than a simple salt and sugar cure. I also prefer to hot smoke my trout for a milder smoky flavor that still allows the flavor of the fish to shine.

Here's how I do it, both ways…

10-12 8-12 oz. trout fillets, skin on
2 cups coarse sea salt
2 cup brown sugar

Cold Smoking

To cure the trout fillets, cover the bottom of a sheet pan with a simple dry cure of 50/50 coarse sea salt to brown sugar, lay on the fillets, and cover with the remaining cure, adding a little more of the mixture to the thick end of the fillets, to balance the curing. Cover with plastic-wrap and refrigerate overnight. Rinse fillets thoroughly, and pat dry with a paper towel.

Return the fillets to the fridge for 4-6 hours to develop the sticky pellicle (which is what the smoke sticks to.) Cold smoke for 8 hours, using alder or pecan, then wrap the fillets in brown paper and allow to sit in the fridge overnight to mellow.

Hot Smoking

Use the same 50/50 dry cure and instructions, and hot smoke at a box temp of 170F (1 chimney) for an hour.

My Favorite Smoked Oysters

1 dozen medium oysters	¼ cup maple syrup
¼ cup soy sauce	6 Tbs light brown sugar

Brine:

2 cups water, tepid	½ Tsp Tabasco
3 cups water	1 Tbs lemon juice

In a large non-metal bowl, whisk syrup, soy sauce, brown sugar, 2 cups water, and Tabasco.

Poach oysters in 3 cups water and lemon juice, about 3 minutes.

Transfer hot oysters into brine. Cover and chill 12 hours.

One hour before smoking, remove oysters from brine, place on cookie sheet and chill 1 hour.

Smoke at 225F, with Alder, for an hour and 45 minutes

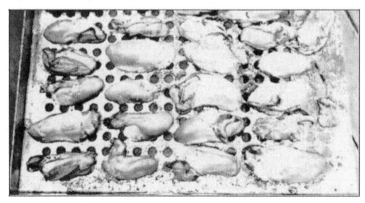

Serve on crackers, in dips, or over pizza. To store, place oysters in an air-tight container and cover with olive oil.

Garlic-Butter Smoked Oysters

2 doz. med fresh oysters, in shell
¼ cup Tillamook butter
1 tsp minced garlic
1 tsp lemon pepper

Combine butter, garlic, and lemon pepper in pan. Heat until simmering, stirring often, remove from heat and set aside.

Heat grill to med-high and scrub oysters under cold water with a wire brush.

Place oysters, cup side down*, on grill and cover.

Cook oysters 5-8 minutes, checking periodically. When an oyster has "popped" (the lid of the shell has opened, remove the oyster from the grill and set aside until cool enough to handle.

Move grilled oysters to into the box, and smoke under medium heat with mesquite, for 15-20 minutes.

Remove the lid of each shell, cutting the oyster loose if necessary.

Drizzle on teaspoon of seasoned butter over the oysters, place cooked oyster in cup of shell, with about ½ of the remaining liquor. and return to the grill.

Cover and allow to cook 10-15 minutes.

Finished oysters will be a deep grey and brown and blackened edges.

Remove from grill and allow to cool until the shells can be handled. Serve with additional lemon-pepper garlic butter.

Notes:

Re-grilling the oysters at a low heat with butter infuses them with a rich, nutty flavor that is completely unlike the taste of a "once cooked" oyster.

Tip: To make a unique and delicious spread, use chilled smoked oysters in your favorite cream-cheese based oyster spread recipe.

To keep oysters upright on the grill, roll tinfoil into 1-inch diameter tubes and make a ring for each oyster to set in.

Sake-Soy Mussels

The recipe was inspired by (*and only slightly modified*) from Andrew Zimmern's Manila Clams with Soy Butter.

Mussels steam-smoked with sake, soy, ginger, chilies, and sugar. Then tossed in a butter-broth reduction. Best mussels I've ever eaten!

- 1 cup sake
- 1/4 cup sugar
- 2 Tbs. garlic-chili sauce
- 1 stick unsalted butter, cubed

1/4 cup soy sauce
1 Tbs. ginger powder
2 lbs. mussels, scrubbed
Salt

Scrub the mussels in cold running water.

In a sauce pan combine the sake, soy sauce, sugar, ginger powder, and chili sauce. Bring just to a boil, whisking to dissolve the sugar. Pour into a large disposable steam pan,

Add the mussels, place the pan in the bottom of the box, and hot smoke with alder wood for 10 minutes. Open the box and shake the pan, repeat every 10 minutes until the mussels open.

Remove the pan from the box and, using a slotted spoon, transfer the mussels to a large bowl; discard any clams that do not open.

Add the butter to the pan, return to box, and allow to smoke until butter is melted. Pour the broth into a saucepan, and bring to a boil over high heat, whisking until incorporated.

Add a dash or two of salt, then pour the sauce over the clams, toss to combine, and serve immediately with toasted French bread and ice-cold sake.

Mardi Gras Cajun BBQ Shrimp

- 3 lbs. head on, unpeeled, deveined shrimp   3 Tbs. Cajun seasoning
- 1 Tbs. extra virgin olive oil

Sauce

- 6 Tbs. (3/4 stick) butter   4 scallions, thinly sliced
- ¼ cup bourbon   ¼ C pilsner beer
- 1 C sweet BBQ sauce   1/3 C heavy whipping cream
- 1 Tbs. Louisiana-style hot sauce Sea salt & freshly ground black pepper

Rinse the shrimp in cold water, drain, and pat dry with paper towels. In a large bowl, toss shrimp with Cajun seasoning, and olive oil.

Preheat Caja China to 250°F.

Arrange the shrimp in a single layer on an oiled grilling grate. and place in the box. Smoke the shrimp with alder wood until firm and bronzed with smoke,   30 to 45 minutes.

Sauce: In a skillet, Melt half of the butter over medium-high heat.

Add half of the scallions and sauté, stirring until just beginning to brown.

Stir in the bourbon and beer and simmer until reduced by half. Add the barbecue sauce and brown sugar, and simmer for another minute. Add the heavy cream, the rest of the butter, and the hot sauce and simmer until thick (about 5 minutes).

Season with salt and pepper to taste.

Remove the smoked shrimp from the box, and toss with the barbecue sauce. Sprinkle with remaining scallion greens or fresh cilantro (opt).

A quick char on your veggies adds tons of flavor to soups, sauces, and other dishes!
Grilled tomatoes, onions and bell peppers will really take your dish to the next level!

VEGGIES

Mock Brisket
Smoked Portobello Mushroom Caps

Portobello mushrooms, with their meaty, musky flavor and dense, slightly chewy consistency, lend themselves perfectly to smoke and barbeque flavors, as they compliment both, without being overwhelmed.

- 2 large portobello mushroom (caps)   1 Tbs apple cider vinegar
- 2 tsp brisket rub   2 Tbs sweet bbq sauce
- Oak wood chunks or chips

Clean mushrooms, brush the gill-side with vinegar, and sprinkle with rub.

Let sit 10-15 minutes.

Place mushrooms in the box, gill-side down, & smoke 30 minutes, at a box temp of 250F.

Flip mushrooms and brush lightly with sauce.

Smoke for an additional hour.

Now, here's the secret... The cup-side of the mushroom didn't get any "char" during smoking, so brush it with a little extra sauce and put it directly above the hottest part of the fire for just a few seconds. You want a little char to simulate the "burnt end" goodness of properly smoked brisket.

Remove mushrooms from the grill and let cool 2-3 minutes gill-side down, on a rack. Slice ½ inch thick on a bias, and serve on white bread with a drizzle of warm sauce, just like you would brisket. To turn this into a killer "brisket" sandwich, add: 2 slice smoked Gouda cheese, as soon as you take them off the grill (*or smoked mozzarella, or smoked cheddar*), and toast two soft Kaiser rolls.

Smoky Russet Potato Pie

This is a favorite from my childhood, and my father's Southern roots, it was always part of our Thanksgiving meal plan.

If you're making this dish *after* a holiday, like maybe *Easter,* and you have some leftover baked ham, sprinkle 1/2 cup of finely chopped ham between each layer, and use some sharp or extra sharp cheddar) to turn this delicious side dish into an amazing entree!

• 1 9" pie crust	3/4 cup heavy cream
• 1 large garlic clove, peeled	1 1/4 pounds russet potatoes
• 2 Tbsp. chopped fresh thyme	1/4 cup chopped parsley
• 1 cube of butter	1 cup heavy cream
• Salt	Black Pepper
• Granulated garlic	1/2 cup grated Gruyère
• ½ cup shredded asiago	2 cups chopped ham (*optional*)

Combine cheeses and set aside.

Peel and slice potatoes as thinly as possible. Bring a pot of heavily salted water to boil and blanch the potatoes for 3-4 minutes. Drain, and place potatoes an ice-water bath to stop cooking. Drain and spread on paper towels. Pat dry.

Place potato slices, in a single layer, on a rack in the bottom of the box, sprinkle with sea salt, and cold smoke, with mesquite, for 1 hour.

Position rack in center of oven and preheat to 350°F.

Arrange 1/3 of the smoked potato rounds, slightly overlapping, in concentric circles in the bottom of the pie crust; sprinkle with salt, pepper, and garlic, then 1/3 of the parsley and thyme, and 1/4 cup of cheese blend.

Dot with teaspoons of butter, and pour 1/4 cup cream over all.

Repeat layering 2 more times with remaining potato, thyme, salt, pepper, garlic, cheese, and cream.

Pour remaining cream over all, and top with remaining cheese.

Bake gratin until golden on top and potatoes are very tender, 1 hour to 1 hour 10 minutes.

If the pie crust becomes too brown, cover with edges with a ring of foil.

Let potato pie rest 10 minutes before serving.

Enjoy!

Baby Potatoes & Camp Hash

I like to use a mix of white, red and purple baby potatoes. They have a thin skin that really lets the smoke permeate, a rich fresh taste, and a velvety tender finish when smoked.

- 1 ½ lb. Baby Potatoes
- ¼ cup Parmesan, grated
- ½ cup fresh chopped Italian parsley
- 2 Tbs. sweet cream butter, melted

Marinade

- ¼ cup olive oil
- ½ tsp. dried basil
- 1 tsp. sea salt
- ½ tsp. coarse black pepper

6 garlic cloves, chopped
½ tsp. dried dill
1 tsp. dried Italian seasoning
½ tsp. red pepper flake (opt)

Combine marinade and potatoes in a large zip-bag and marinate potatoes 24 hours, flipping the bag a couple of times.

OPTIONAL: *Grill the potatoes briefly over direct heat on all sides before smoking, just to get a few spots of char.*

Fire and spread on chimney of coals to bring the box temp to 225 degrees. Smoke potatoes on a rack inside the box for 90 minutes.

Move the potatoes to the large piece of aluminum foil and wrap to make a pouch.

Return to box, and smoke for another hour.

Carefully open the pouch and pour the potatoes into a large bowl and toss with melted butter.

Top with Parmesan and chopped parsley.

Chef's Note:

These potatoes are amazing just as they are, but my favorite way to use them is in my camp breakfast hash!

Combine equal amounts (by cup) of smoked potatoes (cubed) smoked andouille sausage, and a couple of chopped sweet onions and bell peppers, sautéed, in a pan or skillet with ½ cup of your favorite beer.

Cover with foil (poke a few small holes in it) and bake 30 minutes at 350F. If cooking on a camp stove, or fire, lift the foil and stir every few minutes.

Garlic-Butter Corn on the Cob

- 8 ears sweet corn (*with husks*)
- 1 tsp. minced fresh garlic
- ¼ C grated Parmesan cheese

½ C sweet-cream butter
½ C seasoned salt
2 Tbs. chives, chopped

Soak corn, un-shucked, in cold water for 30 minutes.

Combine the butter, garlic and salt in a saucepan over medium heat, stirring until melted; set aside.

Gently peel back the husks, remove the silk, and lay on racks in the bottom of the box. Cold smoke for 1 hour, with mesquite wood.

Remove corn from the box and brush the ears with ½ of the seasoned butter.

Re-cover the corn with the husks and tie each closed with a couple of loops of kitchen string (opt).

Grill corn at over high heat for 30 minutes, turning often.

Shuck each eat, drizzle with remaining butter, sprinkle with cheese, chives, and serve.

Applewood Acorn Squash

- 3 acorn squash (halved & seeded)
- ¼ C butter
- ½ C Saigon cinnamon
- 1 tsp. nutmeg

¼ C brown sugar
3 tsp. grapeseed oil
1 tsp. chili powder

Brush the insides (*cut side*) of the squash with oil. Cover with foil, poking several holes in the top.

Place squash in the box, on a rack cut-side down and smoke with apple-wood at a box temp of 225F for 1 hour.

Melt butter, sugar, and spices in a saucepan. Lift the foil and brush ½ of the butter mixture evenly on squash, the re-cover.

Smoke another hour. When done cooking, you should be able to push a fork into the squash with almost no resistance.

Remove from box, brush with remaining butter mix, and let rest 2-3 minutes before serving.

Chef's Tip: *These are delicious as a side dish, or you can make it a meal by including a sausage stuffing, with ½ lb. Italian sausage, chopped bell pepper, chopped onion, ½ of a jalapeño pepper, and garlic, all sautéed together, and added to the squash (hot) after the first hour of smoking.*

You can also let squash cool, then puree and use them as the base for an amazing smoked acorn squash bisque!

Smoked Brussels Sprouts

- 1 ½ lbs Brussels sprouts
- 2 Tbs. olive oil
- Sea salt and cracked black pepper

2 cloves of garlic minced

2 Tbs. apple-cider vinegar

Trim and rinse the sprouts, and pat dry.

Toss in a large bowl with olive oil, vinegar, garlic, and salt & pepper to taste.

Place the sprouts in a foil-lined pan, in the bottom of the box.

Smoke at a box temp of 25oF for approximately 45 minutes until fork tender.

Optional: I like to toss the finished sprouts on the grill, directly over the fires for a minute or two, just to add a little char.

Up to you.

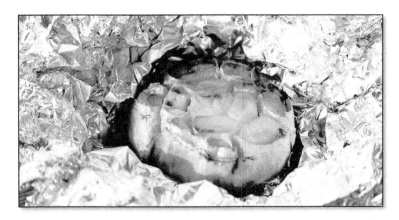

Smoked Garlic

6 heads of garlic, whole
6 Tbs. olive oil
3 tsp. sea salt

Slice the top off each head of garlic to expose the cloves.

In a small bowl, mix the oil, salt, and pepper.

Place each bulb in a small foil packet, and drizzle with oil and spice mixture. Close up the foil loosely around each bulb so the smoke can get in (you can also poke a few holes in the top side.)

Place the foil packs on a sheet pan, set in the bottom of the box, and smoke 1 hour at a box temp between 250°F to 275°F with hickory or mesquite.

You can use the smoked garlic immediately, or vacuum pack each bulb and freeze for later.

RESOURCES

Reheating BBQ

When I BBQ, I always like to cook more than I need.

If I'm doing it for business, I pride myself on never having run out of meat, regardless of how many "unexpected" guests show up.

When cooking for just my family, I just like to have leftovers for the rest of the week!

Now, I have reheated BBQ using just about any method you can imagine, from a high-tech sous-vide machine, to wrapped in foil and tossed in the campfire coals, and after much, much trial and error, I have come to the conclusion that vacuum-sealing and slow-heating in hot water, is the #1 best method for getting back to that "just out of the smoker" flavor and consistency.

Basically, I'm talking about *Sous-vide*. But, if you don't have a Sous-vide cooker, or an immersion circulator, never fear...for this technique, a pot of hot water and some heavy-duty zip bags will work almost as well.

Note: I have noticed that I get more flavorful results if I use a vacuum-sealer, but the zip bags are a close second.

How to do it:

Always allow the cooked meat to come to room temperature BEFORE reheating.

This insures that meats will be able to warm all the way to the center without taking so long that the surface begins to dry out.

If you're using a sauce, brush both sides of the meat with a thin layer, before bagging.

If I'm NOT using sauce, I'll add a few tablespoons of apple juice or broth to the bag.

For brisket and pulled pork, I save the juices that gather in the pan while the meat is resting. I de-fat them overnight, and add them to the bags with the meat, before sealing.

Vacuum seal the bag, or if using zips, press out as much of the air as you can before sealing.

Bring several inches of water to simmer is a pot large enough to hold your ribs, brisket, or whatever. Place the bag in the hot water, turn off the heat, and cover.

Allow the meat to rest in the water for 20 minutes, turning the bag over once. Remove the bag, allow to rest ten minutes on the counter to reabsorb the juices, then open (*carefully*), and serve!

I've used this method flawlessly for pork ribs, beef ribs, pulled pork shoulders and, of course, beef brisket.

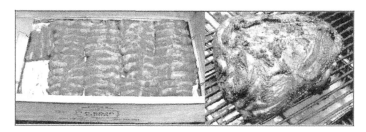

This is a great method for serving left-over bbq while camping, as well, as you can freeze your portions in advance, then just thaw them the day you want to serve and use this method on any camp-stove, or ever over the fire.

For large pieces of meat, like un-pulled pork shoulders, or unsliced brisket, spray the meat generously with apple juice and add 1/4" of juice or broth to the bottom of the pan.

Seal the pan tightly with foil and place in a pre-heated 200°F oven or smoker until warmed to your liking, then slice and serve.

For an extra punch of flavor, you can pre-heat your grill to high, and sear the rested ribs or chicken for a few seconds per side, to re-set the glaze and give it a fresh kiss of fire!

"Left-over" BBQ doesn't have to be dry and washed out.

Make a little extra next time and enjoy it over rice, tossed with pasta, in any number of killer sandwiches, or just straight up!

Make Your Roasting Box BBQ
An Unforgettable Family Event

Ever since the first whole hog got trussed up over a fire, barbecue and grilling have been a staple of North American living.

For many of us, grilling is a routine mealtime activity, while for the most devoted grillers, summer is ruled by massive barbecue parties. But you don't have to choose between boring repetition and crazy get-togethers: every barbecue can and should be an exciting family event.

Here are 3 ways to make your routine evening barbecue a more unique experience:

Remember those "choose your own adventure" stories?

Try foil-wrapped surprise meals to let everyone build their own dinner! Place different combinations of chicken, fish and vegetables, sauces, and spices on the table and let folks build their own foil packets.

These cook in less than 20 minutes and lead to no-mess, lip-smacking results. Everyone will love the surprise element and can easily switch packets.

You can even ask your family for combo suggestions before the barbecue, or draw ingredient names out of a hat to create new dish ideas!

A little variety goes a long way. If you tend to stick to the same old burgers and tube-steaks, why not try grilled pizza or salmon steaks? Similarly, try to mix it up with condiments and seasoning. Sick of ketchup? Try salsa or Teriyaki sauce instead.

Cooking over (*or under*) a bed of glowing coals is fundamental in almost every corner of the world…hope on the Google and find a new culture to inspire your Q!

A BBQ party doesn't have to be rushed. In fact, the deal should be quite the opposite, which should represent a process of slow cooking on low heat…and nothing does low & slow better than a barbeque!

Hanging out around the magic box while your pig is roasting to perfection is a great way to pass some quality time with your family and friends.

Finally…you're not Bobby Flay, and no one's tracking your ratings, or catching every second on film…chill out, have fun, and try being a guest at your own party!

Too many of us get lost in the details of planning the perfect pit-master party and forget to enjoy our friends, family, and delicious food.

Plan dishes that can be prepared in advance, and don't be afraid to hand off some of the grill duties to others so you can walk around with a cool drink yourself!

So…what do YOU do to make a family BBQ fun? Any special recipes, games or traditions that you'd like to share?

Now get out there and enjoy an unforgettable barbecue!

Finding Whole Pigs

The two most reliable places I've found in my area are the Japanese grocery store (I use one called Uwajimaya), and a restaurant supply stores like Cash & Carry, and Restaurant Depot.

Also, check with your local grocery store's butcher (*Safeway, Albertsons, etc*), as sometimes they have access, or at least leads.

The restaurant supply is going to be, by far, your best deal. If you can't find one in a local online search, talk to the owners of a (*non-chain*) restaurant or coffee shop in your area, they should know.

CLEAN UP & MAINTAINENCE TIPS

Grill Grates – flip them over and set them directly onto the remaining coals after cooking. While you're enjoying dinner, any residual gunk will be carbonized and easy to scrub off with a wire brush.

Internal Meat Racks – These don't really get all that messy, but for easiest clean up, spray your grates with a Pam-style spray just before coming in contact with the meat.

Also, the sooner you scrub them down after cooking, the easier it will be.

Smoking/Cooking Chamber – Line with heavy foil to ease cleaning. I scrub the interior of the box with hot soapy water after every use, then spray with a 50/50 bleach water solution and allow to air dry before replacing the lid. If you have a semi-pro, plug the drain hole and pour several gallons of VERY hot water into the chamber, scrub and drain.

Another gallon of hot water to clean out the drain pipe afterward is a good idea, as well.

Green Clean – If you're not a fan of chemical cleaning products, there are a number of "green" cleaners on the market, or you can go old school and pour two cups of vinegar into the spray bottle; add two cups of water, replace the lid on the bottle and shake it vigorously to mix.

Spray the water/vinegar solution on the racks of the grill and the area above and underneath them to saturation.

Let the solution set for 10 minutes, and them scrub the racks with your wire brush and rinse with clear water. Wipe all appropriate surfaces down with a paper towel and high-heat cooking oil after cleaning.

Internal Meat Temps

Food	Doneness	Temp. (F)
Pork		
Shoulder	Sliceable	180
	Sliceable and Pullable	185
	Pullable	195
Pork Chops	Medium-Rare	130
	Medium	140
Tenderloin	Medium-Rare	135
	Medium	140
Sausage Done		170
Beef		
Brisket	Done	210
Beef Steaks	Rare	120
	Medium-Rare	130
	Medium	135
Beef Roasts	Rare	115
	Medium-Rare	125
	Medium	130
Chicken		
Whole/Pieces	Done	170
Cornish Hen	Done	170
Duck	Done	175
Ground Meat	Medium	160
Ham	Pre-Cooked	140
	Not Pre-Cooked	160
Lamb		
Chops/Rack	Rare	120
Turkey		
Breast	Done	165
Dark Meat	Done	175
Veal		
Chops	Medium-Rare	130
Roasts	Medium	135
	Medium-Rare	125
	Medium	130
Venison	Medium	135
	Medium-Rare	125

How to Spatchcock Poultry

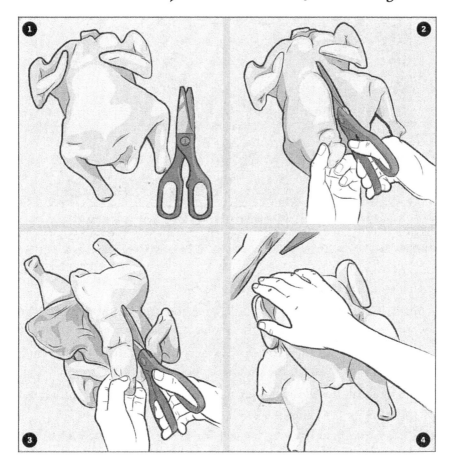

1. Lay the bird breast down.

2. Cut along one side of the spine, from the tail, all the way through.

3. Repeat on the other side and remove the spine (save it for stock!)

4. Flip the bird over and press down on the breast-bone until it cracks, flattening out the bird.

How much is enough? BBQ for a crowd.

One of the most frustrating aspects of cooking for a crowd is the fear of running out of food.

I HATE seeing an empty pan on my serving table!

So, how much should you buy? Too little, and you risk running out, too much and you've spent more than you need to (this looks especially bad to a catering client!)

Here are some general guidelines to help you calculate how many people you can serve with that raw chunk of meat on the butcher's shelf...

When planning a meal, it is always better to purchase too much meat than not enough. Always be prepared for people with larger appetites.

One trick I use is to add a "mystery" guest for every 4 confirmed. In other words, I plan 5 portions for 4 people, 10 portions for 8, 15 for 12, etc. If there are leftovers, the cooked meat will keep in the refrigerator for several days or the unused portions may be frozen for long term storage.

Approximate Pounds Per Person

(Raw weight)

Pork, Shoulder Bone-in	3
Pork, Back Ribs	1.5
Pork, Country Style Ribs	2
Pork, Spareribs	1.5
Pork, Whole	1.5
Beef, Standing Rib	2.5
Beef, Ribs	2.5
Beef, Tri-Tip	4
Chicken, Whole	3
Lamb, Leg (bone in)	1
Turkey, Whole	¾

BBQ Terms Glossary

Chef's Tip: For step-by-step how to videos on these techniques, search "What is" or "How to" followed by the glossary term, on the YouTube homepage.

3-2-1 - A method of smoking that uses 3 hours smoke, 2 hours foiled, 1 hr unwrapped. The foiling helps keep the meat moist and tender.

Baby Back Ribs - Taken from the top of the rib cage between the spine and the spareribs. They are not as large as spare ribs.

Beer Can Chicken - Chicken cooked on rack that holds a whole chicken upright with a can of your favorite liquid inside of the chicken. The can of soda, juice, water or most commonly beer keeps the chicken moist.

Big Drum Smoker - Smoker made from a 55-gallon barrel.

Briquettes - Charcoal that normally contains some additives. Burns longer and cooler than lump. Used for grilling and smoking.

Big Green Egg - Popular brand of a ceramic cooker.

Brine - Water saturated with salt and the meat is marinated in the brine solution. Normally some spices are added to the brine. Through a chemical process, this allows the meat to remain moist during the cook.

Burnt Ends - Flavorful pieces of meat cut from the ends of a smoked brisket and are considered a delicacy in barbecue cooking.

Boston Butt - The upper portion of a pork shoulder. Normally 6-8 pounds and commonly used for pulled pork.

Ceramic Cooker - Very efficient type of grill/smoker. Retains heat very well and capable of very high temperatures.

Chile Grill - A stainless steel rack with holes used to cook whole peppers

Chimney Starter - Looks like a large coffee can with holes and a handle. Allows you to start charcoal without using fluid.

Flat - One of the two cuts of brisket. The flat has has minimal fat and is usually more expensive than the more flavorful point cut.

Grill Marks - Black impressions of the cooking grate that are burned into the meat.

Kansas City Style Ribs - Spareribs that are trimmed even more closely than the St. Louis style ribs, and have the hard bone removed.

Lighter Fluid - Alcohol based chemical used in starting charcoal. Normally gives a chemical taste in the food. Can be dangerous to use

Kettle – A round grill, with a domed lid. Weber is the most well known brand of kettle grills.

Low & Slow - Smoking using low heat. Briskets, roasts, ribs, butts, etc are normally low and slow.

Lump Charcoal - 100% Natural pieces of wood that have been pre-burned to create charcoal. Lump is irregular in shape and burns hotter than briquettes. Used mostly for grilling.

Minion Method - A method created by Jim Minion. Place several lit coals on top of a full chamber of unlit coals. The unlit coals gradually light throughout the cook from the lit coals resulting in a much longer cook time of up to 18 hours depending on conditions.

Mop - Basting liquid added to meat while cooking.

Offset Smoker - A very common type of smoker that has two chambers, a firebox and a cooking chamber.

Packer - A whole brisket that is untrimmed of fat. This keeps the brisket "self basting" during the cook so that it remains moist. Varies in weight from 8 to 20 pounds.

Pellet Smoker - A smoker that uses food-grade wood pellets for fuel instead of charcoal or gas.

Point - One of two cuts of brisket. The point has more fat and flavor than the flat cut.

Rub - Spices that are massaged into the meat prior to cooking for flavoring and to form a crust on the meat.

Searing - A technique used in grilling that cooks the surface of the meat at a high temperature so that a caramelized crust forms. Searing is believed to lock in the natural juices of the meat.

Seasoning Grates - Coating the cooking grate with olive oil just before adding the meat.

Seasoning Grill/Smoker - Coating the entire interior surface of a grill or smoker with cooking oil or spray with Pam and then light a fire and burn for several hours at about 350*. This removes manufacturer coatings and impurities.

Seasoned Wood - Wood that has been split and set aside for 6 months or longer to dry out and use for smoking.

Slather - Normally mustard is used by rubbing a thin layer on the meat so that the rub sticks to the meat and doesnt fall off.

Smoking Wood - Hardwoods that are normally mesquite or fruit woods such as apple, cherry, pear, etc and have been seasoned. Can be in logs, chunks, chips, or pellets.

Spatchcock - A chicken or game bird that is prepared by slicing out the backbone of the chicken and flattening it out prior to cooking over a grill.

Spare Ribs - Spare ribs contain more bone than meat and fat which can make the ribs more tender than back ribs.

Spritz - A thin liquid, normally a fruit juice, beer or even liquor in a spray bottle that is sprayed on the meat during cooking to aid in keeping the meat from drying out.

St. Louis Style Ribs - Spareribs trimmed where the sternum bone, cartilage and rib tips have been removed.

Stick Burner - Smoker that uses whole wood logs for fuel instead of charcoal, gas or pellets

Texas Crutch - Placing a brisket in foil, or butcher paper, to help it remain moist during the smoke

UDS (Ugly Drum Smoker) - An upright smoker made from a 55 gallon barrel.

Upright Smoker - A smoker that uses a vertical smoking chamber. Usually contains several trays that are stacked. Considered a more efficient smoker than a horizontal offset. Firebox is either under the cooking chamber or beside it.

Whole Brisket - Contains both the flat and the point cuts of the brisket.

Yardbird - Slang for a chicken

Index

La Caja China Cooking

The secret to perfect roasting
2018 Edition

Perry P. Perkins

LA CAJA CHINA WORLD

Roasting Box Recipes
from Around the Globe

Perry P. Perkins

LA CAJA CHINA PARTY!

13 Perfect Theme Parties
for making memories
with the Magic Box!

Perry P. Perkins

La Caja China Grill!

Tasting the Flames

Perry P. Perkins

PERRY P. PERKINS

BARBEQUE

A home chef's guide

GRILLING
A home chef's guide

PERRY P. PERKINS

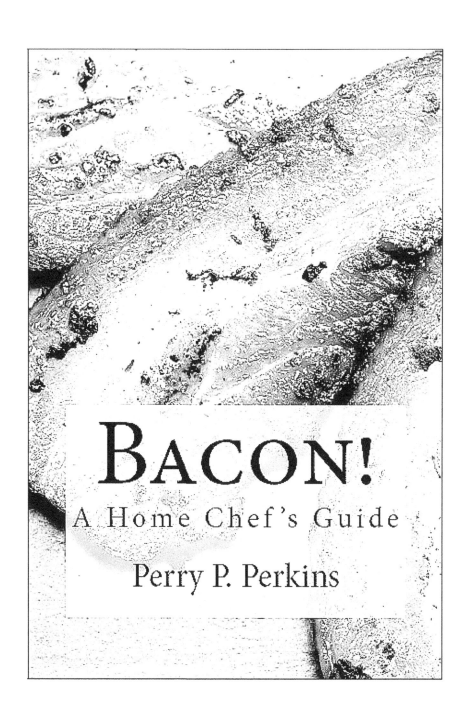

BACON!

A Home Chef's Guide

Perry P. Perkins

Author's Biography

Chef Perry Perkins lives in Washington State, and is a third generation professional chef, an author, and a food blogger.

Perry writes regularly for La Caja China, Latin Touch, Grilling is Happiness, and his own roasting box blog: **www.lacajachinacooking.com**

He also operates SimplySmartDinnerPlans.com, which offers a free weekly recipe and meal-planning service and teaches cooking classes as part of his non-profit's **My Kitchen Outreach Program**, a charity organization that teaches the basics of nutrition and money-saving shopping, as well as hands-on cooking classes for at-risk and under-served youth

More from Chef Perry

Blog

www.chefperryperkins.com

Facebook

www.facebook.com/chefperryperkins/

YouTube Videos

www.homechefvideos.com

Bookstore

www.perryperkinsbooks.com

Have a roasting box question? Email me personally at chefperryp@gmail.com, or contact me at one of the links above. Always happy to help!

~Chef P

Made in the USA
Coppell, TX
01 April 2022

75867014R00122